RILKE

Sonnets to Orpheus

RAINER MARIA
RILKE

*

Sonnets to Orpheus

*

With English Translations
BY C. F. MACINTYRE

University of California Press
Berkeley, Los Angeles, London

University of California Press
Berkeley and Los Angeles, California

© 1960 by C. F. MacIntyre

ISBN: 0-520-01069-8

Library of Congress Catalogue Card No. 60-9649

Designed by Ward Ritchie

Printed in the United States of America

The *Duino Elegies* constitute a massive, earth-based structure, and remind one of Notre-Dame, with its aspirations and its grotesqueries. The slighter *Sonnets to Orpheus* stand to one side, each a definite artifact, reflecting the same architect and material. In fact, the ideas of the Sonnets are often fragments chipped from the rough-hewn Elegies; sometimes they epitomize an elegy, often they develop a corollary from the larger work. Like the Treasury beside the Cathedral, they hoard many rare bijoux, bright esoteric gems not to be put too readily in public view. A series of sonnets is more easily worked with than the slower-moving Elegies, and a reader familiar with the several themes of the Sonnets will discover that the Elegies finally go off with but slight documentation.

Rilke always maintained that this book was from the most mysterious and enigmatic "dictation ever entrusted" to him—and this is both pompous and pontifical. They were written, he continues, "in a single breathless attention . . . without one word's being in doubt or requiring to be altered." This is pure arrogance. "Would to God," as Jonson said of Shakespeare, "he had blotted a thousand!"

The Sonnets were written during some two weeks in February, 1922, the month that saw the completion of the Elegies. In a way, they seem the secundatum thrown off by the greater effort. Readers of Rilke will be familiar with his evasiveness in dealing with their genesis: (1) a young girl, a dancer whom he had seen but once, the daughter of an acquaintance with whom he had never been on intimate terms, died. (2) He had recently acquired a small print of Orpheus playing on the lyre. (3) He had already made translations from the work of Paul Valéry, among them the essay "L'Ame et la danse" and "Le Cimetière marin." That their author had suffered from a long period of poetic lethargy and inaction and had then produced *La Jeune Parque* certainly gave Rilke a profound impetus for the completion of the Elegies and the reception of the "dictation" of the Sonnets.

As a result of this combination he had not only the immediate occasion and the symbol, but the example of a distinguished colleague. In conjunction with one of those inexplicable emotional releases which we call "inspiration," what could be expected from all these focusing forces but the gushing forth of a book?

In Monique Saint-Hélier's *À Rilke pour Noël* (Chandelier, Berne, 1927, p. 21) we find a passage which indicates precisely the debt to Valéry. "I was alone, I was waiting, all my work was within. One day I read Valéry, and I knew that my waiting was at an end." Aside from a few borrowings, the influence was rather one of personality than of imitation.

As to the divine afflatus attending the creation of the Sonnets, opinions are dubious. A.A.M. Stols (Maastricht, 1927, p. 128) writes: "He belongs to that group of creators whose signature should be followed by the name of 'artifex' rather than of 'poeta.'" And Franz Rauhut (*Paul Valéry*, München, 1930, p. 66) writes: "His ecstasy is cold; it is of the intellect rather than of the soul. He cultivated intelligence rather than intuition; he is no mystic, but rather a magic-worker."

After the influence of Rodin, so apparent in *Neue Gedichte*, Rilke was developing into a philosophic poet. He had finished his "work of the eye," as he named it; now was to come the "heart-work." Apparently it was the former which moved Valéry to say to Max Rychner (*Neue Züricher Zeitung*) that he loved in Rilke and *through* Rilke *Dinge*, "Things" (always an especial Rilkean word) which he would not have loved directly for themselves: the occult, the premonitions, intimate appearances of distant things, and the other hitherto secret manifestations of which the German had made him aware. And remember that the speaker was a very hardheaded rationalist.

I must quote the translation of a poem of Valéry's which may also have stimulated the series. Rilke had already translated the poem, which proved a catalytic.

. . . Inspired beneath the myrtles, I create the wonder-
ful Orpheus! From the pure cirque the fire descends,
turns the bald mount to a trophy from which ascends
augustly the act of a god, with ringing thunder.

If the god sings, almightily he breaks
the landscape; the sun sees the horror of moving rocks;
to the dazzling lofty harmonious golden walls
of a sanctuary a unique wailing calls.

Sings Orpheus, sitting beside a sky of fire!
The rock moves, slipping; each enchanted stone
feels a new import, the frenzy for azure light;

evening bathes the half-nude Temple's flight,
and he, mustering himself, in the gold ordains
himself to the vast soul of the hymn on the lyre!

The two Narcissus poems of Valéry influenced Sonnets II, 2 and 3, on mirrors. Other influences have been pointed out in the notes to specific poems. And the young Symbolists grouped around Mallarmé taught Rilke some verse tricks, notably the short-lined un-Germanic sonnet.

From the many loose lines, fragments from the Elegies collecting for ten years, Rilke, with the various influences and the impetus mentioned above, finally burst over, like a volcano, and wrote the series in too short a time. But he certainly gave himself airs about their creation which are very irritating. He wrote several melodramatic letters, for all the world like the complaints of a hysterical woman in an interesting situation, about the spiritual tempest that threatened to rend his whole being, et cetera. ("Look, sir, I bleed!" as the bastard said to Gloucester.) He had moaned and groaned in whole nights of agony. One prefers Dante's litotic assertion that the writing of the *Commedia* had kept him lean.

Rilke seems always to have needed a spiritual prop, as a morning-glory vine drapes itself around a pump handle overnight. Earlier he had worshiped Jacobsen and Tolstoy. Rodin had given him the clear objective way of seeing that produced *Neue Gedichte*. Valéry's self-discipline after a long silence had encouraged him to overcome the apathy of a dozen years. A friend had lent him a small castle at Muzot. A couple of elderly noblewomen kept him in groceries and coddled him. He had wonderful days among his roses and grand long nights of solitude. His style had changed completely in the interim.

In evidence, let me quote "Spanische Tänzerin" (*N.G.*) for comparison with Sonnets I, 15, and II, 18.

As in the hand a match glows, swiftly white
before it bursts in flame and to all sides
licks its quivering tongues: within the ring
of spectators her wheeling dance is bright,
nimble, and fervid, twitches and grows wide.

And suddenly is made of pure fire.

Now her glances kindle the dark hair;
she twirls the floating skirts with daring art
into a whirlwind of consuming flame,
from which her naked arms alertly strike,
clattering like fearful rattlesnakes.

Then, as the fire presses her too closely,
imperiously she clutches it and throws it
with haughty gestures to the floor and watches
it rage and leap with flames that will not die—
until, victorious, surely, with a sweet
greeting smile, and holding her head high,
she tramples it to death with small, firm feet.

Here we find a visual, sculptural treatment which
freezes one art into another with its cold fire. It
is as objective and clear-cut as a Manet painting.
There are no further implications to be drawn
from it. We are shown none of the poet's per-
sonal feelings about the woman. As a matter of
fact, she was an entertainer at a wedding party, for
the daughter of Zuloaga.

Now, if the reader will look at I, 15, where the little girl is invited to "dance the orange," and then at I, 25, second quatrain: "A dancer first, then her hesitant body stood / suddenly, as if youth were cast in bronze," and then compare II, 18, he can see how the poet's mind and technique had altered in the fifteen years between the two books. Here the girl is no longer merely a dancer; she has become the symbol of metamorphosis, "a transition of all transciency into action." All the summer and sunlight, all the practice of the "hard-won year," have been suddenly drawn together and expressed in an achieved gesture, and now it rests for an instant, static as a "tree of rapture." Then is added a pitcher and vase, and a final figure of the turning on a potter's wheel. Certainly this lacks the unity of the poem about the Spanish dancer, but one feels here that Rilke was searching for something beyond ordinary human ken.

Just as Blake used much of the same subject-matter in his two books of songs, Rilke re-creates many of the earlier objectively treated poems of N.G.: gardens, fountains, temples, dogs, children, beggars, trees, figs, pitchers, and rings, but now they are all used figuratively, as symbols. Aside from the pieces on the little white Russian horse, the fabulous unicorn, the dog and the slain doves, the fine animal poems of the earlier books seem to have been forgotten, or, rather, deliberately superseded. The only flowers specifically mentioned now are the anemone and the rose.

But whatever one may think of the matter, the technique of the poet is still masterly. He has not yet got over early French influences, and the same maddeningly perverse yet compelling phrases and arabesques are to be found here. Every critic of Rilke has called him a man of nuances, i.e., a dealer in delicate shadings, tones slightly off-key, and ironically employed expressions. His ability as a musician of verse is commented on in a score of books, but, better than that, it is immediately apparent if the poems are read aloud. His work is deeply indebted to, or else marvelously akin to, the ideal pattern set forth in Verlaine's "Art poétique" which was a bible for the younger Symbolists.

You must have music first of all,
and for that a rhythm uneven is best,
vague as the air and soluble,
with nothing heavy and nothing at rest. . . .

Never the Color, always the Shade,
always the nuance is supreme! . . .

Let there be music, again and forever! . . .
and all the rest is literature.

The last word here, of course, is used pejoratively.

I do not wish to seem unaware of many poetic shortcomings and sins on Rilke's part. The following examples could be multiplied invidiously. But no one should write: ". . . daß sie völlig voll-

ziehst . . ." or ". . . singender steige . . ." or
he is not writing good German. When he asks
the dancer to "create the relation . . . with the
juice that brims this happy thing" (an orange!),
or exclaims: ". . . see in the dish / how odd are
the faces of fish," Erato has been nodding on
Parnassus.

A word about the form of the sonnets. There
are two or three examples in almost Petrarchan
form, notably I, 4 and 17, where the octaves are
built on two rhymes; the rest employ quatrains
unjoined by similar rhymes, and all the sestets
have the usual half-dozen variations. He has ex-
perimented with different line lengths and meters,
not always successfully. Line 8 in II, 17 has
twenty badly digested syllables, most of which
seem to have been hauled along on a trailer in
case something broke down. Many of the sonnets
use lines of varying lengths and the effect is
choppy. His sonnets in pentameter go off much
better than his short-liners, a type borrowed from
the French Symbolists. Two of his best, II, 4 and
15, are built on hard masculine monosyllabic
rhymes. I have, as usual, reduced the character-
istic feminine rhymes natural to the German lan-
guage to my own idiom, for the trochaic effect
bores the English ear. Too many translators feel
obligated to reproduce the exact German meter,
and their verses abound in silly double-rhymes as
bad as an overuse of "voluble-soluble, compress-
ible-dressable, awful-crawful," and thousands of
nasty "-ing" rhymes. These sinners have done

Goethe, Rilke, and Stefan George splendid disservice. "May their tribe increase!"

Granted that Pegasus, indubitably a stallion, may be allowed a reasonable number of caracoles, mincings and prancings, turf-tearings, snortings, foistings, and whiffletree gymnastics, he ought not behave like a mustang at a rodeo. In these sonnets Rilke often does just that. He is sometimes as irritating as Hopkins. And, alas! there are no more Urquharts among us.

The best translators seldom afford their readers steeds other than gelded hacks. Such animals should not draw undue attention to their failings; they should walk decently along and not get burs in their tails; they should not raise their voices, lest they sound dangerously like a chorus of asses braying.

Rilke offers plenty of capricious sentences. He invents unnecessary word-endings, telegraphs his style. He manufactures adverbs from adjectives that resent it, and he uses adjectives, vague enough at best, as nouns which remain almost untranslatable. I have tried to avoid creating English inanities as potential equivalents of his fatuous idiosyncrasies.

A bibliography of major debts was included in *Rainer Maria Rilke*, Berkeley, 1940. At present I must add M. D. Herter Norton's prose versions, and the notes of the translations of J. B. Leishman which have been particularly helpful. For readers of tough German criticism I suggest Eudo C. Mason's *Lebenhaltung und Symbolik bei*

Rainer Maria Rilke, Weimar, 1939, and Hans
Egon Holthusen's *Rilkes Sonette an Orpheus,
Versuch einer Interpretation*, München, 1937. I
have profited by the French translations of J.-F.
Angelloz, Aubier, 1943, and of Maurice Betz,
Émile-Paul, Paris, 1942. They both made linear
translations without attempting to reduce the
results to verse, but Rilke goes awkwardly into
French prose.

And now let the reader believe Mason's "Alles
Gedankliche hat aber in den Sonetten, ohne
dadurch entwertet zu werden, eine Art musikal-
ische Verflüssigung erfahren," and let him start
his first reading—it will take him several.

C.F.M.

*Weimar, San Francisco, Paris
1938–1959*

Da stieg ein Baum. O reine Übersteigung!
O Orpheus singt! O hoher Baum im Ohr!
Und alles schwieg. Doch selbst in der
    Verschweigung
ging neuer Anfang, Wink und Wandlung vor.

Tiere aus Stille drangen aus dem klaren
gelösten Wald von Lager und Genist;
und da ergab sich, daß sie nicht aus List
und nicht aus Angst in sich so leise waren,

sondern aus Hören. Brüllen, Schrei, Geröhr
schien klein in ihren Herzen. Und wo eben
kaum eine Hütte war, dies zu empfangen,

ein Unterschlupf aus dunkelstem Verlangen
mit einem Zugang, dessen Pfosten beben,—
da schufst du ihnen Tempel im Gehör.

1

There arose a tree. Oh, pure transcension!
Oh, Orpheus sings! Oh, tall tree in the ear!
And all was still. But even in this suspension
new beginnings, signs, and changes were.

Animals from the silence, from the clear
now opened wood came forth from nest and den;
and it so came to pass that not from fear
or craftiness were they so quiet then,

but to be listening. Howling, cry, roar
seemed little to their hearts. Where scarce a
    humble
hut for such reception was before,

a hiding-place of the obscurest yearning,
with entrance shaft whose underpinnings tremble,
you made for the beasts temples in the hearing.

Und fast ein Mädchen wars und ging hervor
aus diesem einigen Glück von Sang und Leier
und glänzte klar durch ihre Frühlingsschleier
und machte sich ein Bett in meinem Ohr.

Und schlief in mir. Und alles war ihr Schlaf.
Die Bäume, die ich je bewundert, diese
fühlbare Ferne, die gefühlte Wiese
und jedes Staunen, das mich selbst betraf.

Sie schlief die Welt. Singender Gott, wie hast
du sie vollendet, daß sie nicht begehrte,
erst wach zu sein? Sieh, sie erstand und schlief.

Wo ist ihr Tod? O, wirst du dies Motiv
erfinden noch, eh sich dein Lied verzehrte?—
Wo sinkt sie hin aus mir? . . . Ein Mädchen
  fast . . .

She was almost a girl and forth she leaped
from this harmonious joy of song and lyre,
shining through her springtime veils and clear,
she made herself a bed in my ear. And slept

in me. Her sleep was everything. The trees
that I had always loved so much, and these
palpable distances, the field I felt,
and each amazement that to me befell.

She slept the world. Ah, singing god, how have
you so perfected her, she did not crave
to waken first? She rose and fell asleep.

Where is her death? Before your song is lost,
can you not find this motif? To what deeps
does she sink from me—where? . . . A girl
    almost . . .

Ein Gott vermags. Wie aber, sag mir, soll
ein Mann ihm folgen durch die schmale Leier?
Sein Sinn ist Zwiespalt. An der Kreuzung zweier
Herzwege steht kein Tempel für Apoll.

Gesang, wie du ihn lehrst, ist nicht Begehr,
nicht Werbung um ein endlich noch Erreichtes;
Gesang ist Dasein. Für den Gott ein Leichtes.
Wann aber sind wir? Und wann wendet er

an unser Sein die Erde und die Sterne?
Dies ists nicht, Jüngling, daß du liebst, wenn
    auch
die Stimme dann den Mund dir aufstößt,—lerne

vergessen, daß du aufsangst. Das verrinnt.
In Wahrheit singen, ist ein andrer Hauch.
Ein Hauch um nichts. Ein Wehn im Gott. Ein
    Wind.

3

A god can do it. But how shall a man, say,
get to him through the narrow lyre and follow?
His mind's dichotomy. Where two heartways
cross there stands no temple for Apollo.

Song, as you explain it, is not passion,
not striving for some end at last attained;
song is Being. Easy for gods to fashion.
But when shall we *be*? And when will he bend

the earth and stars upon our being? Youth,
it *is* not that you are in love; although
the voice bursts your mouth open, you must find

how to forget your rash song. That will go.
It is another breath that sings the truth.
A breath round nothing. A gust in the god. A
   wind.

O ihr Zärtlichen, tretet zuweilen
in den Atem, der euch nicht meint,
laßt ihn an eueren Wangen sich teilen,
hinter euch zittert er, wieder vereint.

O ihr Seligen, o ihr Heilen,
die ihr der Anfang der Herzen scheint.
Bogen der Pfeile und Ziele von Pfeilen,
ewiger glänzt euer Lächeln verweint.

Fürchtet euch nicht zu leiden, die Schwere,
gebt sie zurück an der Erde Gewicht;
schwer sind die Berge, schwer sind die Meere.

Selbst die als Kinder ihr pflanztet, die Bäume,
wurden zu schwer längst; ihr trüget sie nicht.
Aber die Lüfte . . . aber die Räume . . .

O you tender ones, sometimes walk
into the breath not intended for you;
let it divide against your cheeks,
behind you it trembles, joined anew.

O you blessèd, whole ones, you
who seem to be the beginning of hearts.
Bows for arrows, targets for darts,
more everlasting your smile shines through

the tears. Don't fear to suffer pain;
give the heaviness back to earth's weight again;
heavy are mountains, heavy the seas.

Those you planted as children, ah, those trees
are long since too heavy for you to bear.
But the spaces . . . but the windy air . . .

Errichtet keinen Denkstein. Laßt die Rose
nur jedes Jahr zu seinen Gunsten blühn.
Denn Orpheus ists. Seine Metamorphose
in dem und dem. Wir sollen uns nicht mühn

um andre Namen. Ein für alle Male
ists Orpheus, wenn es singt. Er kommt und geht.
Ists nicht schon viel, wenn er die Rosenschale
um ein paar Tage manchmal übersteht?

O wie er schwinden muß, daß ihrs begrifft!
Und wenn ihm selbst auch bangte, daß er
    schwände.
Indem sein Wort das Hiersein übertrifft,

ist er schon dort, wohin ihrs nicht begleitet.
Der Leier Gitter zwängt ihm nicht die Hände.
Und er gehorcht, indem er überschreitet.

Erect no monument. But let the roses
blossom every year for his memory's sake.
For it is Orpheus. His metamorphosis
into this one and that. We need not take

trouble for other names. Once and for all,
it's Orpheus when there's song. He comes and
    goes.
Is it not much if sometimes a few days
he outlives the roses in the bowl?

He has to vanish, so you'll understand:
Even though himself he fears this evanescence.
For while his word surpasses this existence,

he's gone alone already in the distance.
The lyre's grating does not curb his hands.
He is obedient, even when he transgresses.

Ist er ein Hiesiger? Nein, aus beiden
Reichen erwuchs seine weite Natur.
Kundiger böge die Zweige der Weiden,
wer die Wurzeln der Weiden erfuhr.

Geht ihr zu Bette, so laßt auf dem Tische
Brot nicht und Milch nicht; die Toten ziehts—.
Aber er, der Beschwörende, mische
unter der Milde des Augenlids

ihre Erscheinung in alles Geschaute;
und der Zauber von Erdrauch und Raute
sei ihm so wahr wie der klarste Bezug.

Nichts kann das gültige Bild ihm verschlimmern;
sei es aus Gräbern, sei es aus Zimmern,
rühme er Fingerring, Spange und Krug.

Does he belong here? No, from both
realms his ample nature has grown.
One to whom the roots were known
could bend more deftly the willow's growth.

Never leave milk on the table or bread
when you go to sleep; that lures the dead.
But let him who conjures them to rise,
under the gentle lids of his eyes

mix their ghosts with all he perceives;
may the spell of fumitory and rue
be real for him as the clearest things.

Nothing impairs the symbol that's true;
be it from houses, be it from graves,
let him praise bracelet, pitcher, and ring.

Rühmen, das ists! Ein zum Rühmen Bestellter,
ging er hervor wie das Erz aus des Steins
Schweigen. Sein Herz, o vergängliche Kelter
eines den Menschen unendlichen Weins.

Nie versagt ihm die Stimme am Staube,
wenn ihn das göttliche Beispiel ergreift.
Alles wird Weinberg, alles wird Traube,
in seinem fühlenden Süden gereift.

Nicht in den Grüften der Könige Moder
straft ihm die Rühmung Lügen, oder
daß von den Göttern ein Schatten fällt.

Er ist einer der bleibenden Boten,
der noch weit in die Türen der Toten
Schalen mit rühmlichen Früchten hält.

Praising, that's it! One ordained to praise,
he sprang like ore from the silence of stone.
His heart, oh, perishable winepress
of an infinite wine, for man alone.

His voice no dust can choke or dim
when divine instance seizes him.
All turns vineyard, clusters of grapes,
in his susceptible south grown ripe.

Nor mold in the kings' sepulchers
gives the lie to his laudings, nor
that from the gods a shadow falls.

Of the abiding messengers,
he reaches far into death's door
glorious fruit in golden bowls.

Nur im Raum der Rühmung darf die Klage
gehn, die Nymphe des geweinten Quells,
wachend über unserm Niederschlage,
daß er klar sei an demselben Fels,

der die Tore trägt und die Altäre.—
Sieh, um ihre stillen Schultern früht
das Gefühl, daß sie die jüngste wäre
unter den Geschwistern im Gemüt.

Jubel weiß, und Sehnsucht ist geständig,—
nur die Klage lernt noch; mädchenhändig
zählt sie nächtelang das alte Schlimme.

Aber plötzlich, schräg und ungeübt,
hält sie doch ein Sternbild unsrer Stimme
in den Himmel, den ihr Hauch nicht trübt.

Only in the land of Praise can Lamentation
work: the guardian nymph of the weeping source,
she watches over our precipitation,
that it run clearly on the rocky base,

the same on which the gates and altars stand.
See, around her tranquil shoulders broods
the dawning feeling: she, of all the band,
is the youngest of the Passions' sisterhood.

Rejoicing *knows*, and Longing is contrite:
only Lament still learns; and night by night
tallies with girlish hands the ancient evil.

But suddenly, unpracticed and awry,
she holds a star-sign of our voices high
against a sky her breathing does not trouble.

Nur wer die Leier schon hob
auch unter Schatten,
darf das unendliche Lob
ahnend erstatten.

Nur wer mit Toten vom Mohn
aß, von dem ihren,
wird nicht den leisesten Ton
wieder verlieren.

Mag auch die Spieglung im Teich
oft uns verschwimmen:
Wisse das Bild.

Erst in dem Doppelbereich
werden die Stimmen
ewig und mild.

Euch, die ihr nie mein Gefühl verließt,
grüß ich, antikische Sarkophage,
die das fröhliche Wasser römischer Tage
als ein wandelndes Lied durchfließt.

Oder jene so offenen, wie das Aug
eines frohen erwachenden Hirten,
—innen voll Stille und Bienensaug—
denen entzückte Falter entschwirrten;

alle, die man dem Zweifel entreißt,
grüß ich, die wiedergeöffneten Munde,
die schon wußten, was schweigen heißt.

Wissen wirs, Freunde, wissen wirs nicht?
Beides bildet die zögernde Stunde
in dem menschlichen Angesicht.

Antique sarcophagi, who have never
left my feelings, I greet you, from whom
the joyous waters of days in Rome
flow as a wandering song forever.

Or you so open, like the eyes
of a happy awakening shepherd: tombs
full of silence and dead-nettle bloom,
whence fluttered enchanted butterflies;

all who are delivered from doubt,
I greet, the mouths now open anew,
already aware what silence means.

Do we know it, friends, or do we not?
The lingering hour molds these two
on the countenance of man.

Sieh den Himmel. Heißt kein Sternbild „Reiter"?
Denn dies ist uns seltsam eingeprägt:
dieser Stolz aus Erde. Und ein zweiter,
der ihn treibt und hält und den er trägt.

Ist nicht so, gejagt und dann gebändigt,
diese sehnige Natur des Seins?
Weg und Wendung. Doch ein Druck verständigt.
Neue Weite. Und die zwei sind eins.

Aber sind sie's? Oder meinen beide
nicht den Weg, den sie zusammen tun?
Namenlos schon trennt sie Tisch und Weide.

Auch die sternische Verbindung trügt.
Doch uns freue eine Weile nun,
der Figur zu glauben. Das genügt.

Look at the sky. Is there no constellation
called "Horseman"? For this pride from earth
   we bear,
strangely engraven. And a second's there,
who rides and spurs and guides its destination.

Is not this being whipped and then restrained
like our existence, the sinew and the bone?
Highway and turning. But a touch explains.
New open vistas. And the two are one.

But *are* they that? Or do not they both mean
the road they go together? Then between,
the utter separation of table and trough.

Even stellar conjunctions can deceive.
But let us rejoice a short time to believe
the figure as a symbol. That's enough.

Heil dem Geist, der uns verbinden mag;
denn wir leben wahrhaft in Figuren.
Und mit kleinen Schritten gehn die Uhren
neben unserm eigentlichen Tag.

Ohne unsern wahren Platz zu kennen,
handeln wir aus wirklichem Bezug.
Die Antennen fühlen die Antennen,
und die leere Ferne trug . . .

Reine Spannung. O Musik der Kräfte!
Ist nicht durch die läßlichen Geschäfte
jede Störung von dir abgelenkt?

Selbst wenn sich der Bauer sorgt und handelt,
wo die Saat in Sommer sich verwandelt,
reicht er niemals hin. Die Erde schenkt.

12

Hail to the spirit that can unite us;
for we live really in figures. Always
go the clocks with little strides
along with our intrinsic days.

Without knowing our proper place,
we act as if from true relations.
The antennae feel their sister-stations,
and the emptiness of space

bore . . . pure tension. O music of forces!
Aren't the interruptions turned away
by the indulgent affairs of the day?

However the peasant works and sows,
he never reaches those deep sources
where seeds turn into summer. Earth *bestows.*

Voller Apfel, Birne und Banane,
Stachelbeere . . . Alles dieses spricht
Tod und Leben in den Mund . . . Ich ahne . . .
Lest es einem Kind vom Angesicht,

wenn es sie erschmeckt. Dies kommt von weit.
Wird euch langsam namenlos im Munde?
Wo sonst Worte waren, fließen Funde,
aus dem Fruchtfleisch überrascht befreit.

Wagt zu sagen, was ihr Apfel nennt.
Diese Süße, die sich erst verdichtet,
um, im Schmecken leise aufgerichtet,

klar zu werden, wach und transparent,
doppeldeutig, sonnig, erdig, hiesig—:
O Erfahrung, Fühlung, Freude—, riesig!

Full-plumped apple, gooseberry and pear,
banana . . . all these speak
death and life in the mouth . . . I divine there . . .
read it on a child's cheek

who tastes them. This comes from afar. Will it be
in the mouth something nameless, slow?
Where words were once, discoveries flow,
out of the fruit's flesh, surprised and set free.

Dare to say what you name Apple. This
sweetness, first condensing, thus
gently created in the taste,

becomes awake, transparent, clear,
ambiguous, sunny, earthy, here—
oh, experience, feeling, joy—how vast!

Wir gehen um mit Blume, Weinblatt, Frucht.
Sie sprechen nicht die Sprache nur des Jahres.
Aus Dunkel steigt ein buntes Offenbares
und hat vielleicht den Glanz der Eifersucht

der Toten an sich, die die Erde stärken.
Was wissen wir von ihrem Teil an dem?
Es ist seit lange ihre Art, den Lehm
mit ihrem freien Marke zu durchmärken.

Nun fragt sich nur: tun sie es gern? . . .
Drängt diese Frucht, ein Werk von schweren
    Sklaven,
geballt zu uns empor, zu ihren Herrn?

Sind sie die Herrn, die bei den Wurzeln schlafen,
und gönnen uns aus ihren Überflüssen
dies Zwischending aus stummer Kraft und Küssen?

14

We have to do with flower, grape leaf, fruit.
They speak not only the language of the year.
Out of the dark a pied display appears,
perhaps by the envy of those underfoot

made bright: the dead who give earth strength
  anew.
How do we know what part they make their
  own?
This long time they have larded through and
  through
the clay, with the frank marrow of their bones.

Now arises the question: if this is
gladly done? This work of sullen slaves,
does this globed fruit press toward us, their
  lords?

Are *they* the masters, in their rooty graves
sleeping, who grant from their abundant
  hoards
this mongrel begotten of dumb strength and
  kisses?

Wartet . . . , das schmeckt . . . Schon ists auf
   der Flucht.
. . . Wenig Musik nur, ein Stampfen, ein
   Summen—:
Mädchen, ihr warmen, Mädchen, ihr stummen,
tanzt den Geschmack der erfahrenen Frucht!

Tanzt die Orange. Wer kann sie vergessen,
wie sie, ertrinkend in sich, sich wehrt
wider ihr Süßsein. Ihr habt sie besessen.
Sie hat sich köstlich zu euch bekehrt.

Tanzt die Orange. Die wärmere Landschaft,
werft sie aus euch, daß die reife erstrahle
in Lüften der Heimat! Erglühte, enthüllt

Düfte um Düfte! Schafft die Verwandtschaft
mit der reinen, sich weigernden Schale,
mit dem Saft, der die glückliche füllt!

15

Wait . . . that tastes good . . . It flies away fast.
. . . Just a bit of music, a trampling, a humming:
girls, you warm, you silent girls coming,
dance the taste of the fruit you test!

Dance the orange. Who can forget it,
how it drowns in itself, yet strives *not* to do
what makes it sweet! Now you have got it:
exquisitely, it has become you.

Dance the orange. The warmer land,
project from you, so this ripe fruit glisten
in its native air! Oh, ardently fling

off fragrance on fragrance. Create the relation
with the pure, the unyielding rind,
with the juice that brims this happy thing!

Du, mein Freund, bist einsam, weil . . .
Wir machen mit Worten und Fingerzeigen
uns allmählich die Welt zu eigen,
vielleicht ihren schwächsten, gefährlichsten Teil.

Wer zeigt mit Fingern auf einen Geruch?—
Doch von den Kräften, die uns bedrohten,
fühlst du viele . . . Du kennst die Toten,
und du erschrickst vor dem Zauberspruch.

Sieh, nun heißt es zusammen ertragen
Stückwerk und Teile, als sei es das Ganze.
Dir helfen, wird schwer sein. Vor allem: pflanze

mich nicht in dein Herz. Ich wüchse zu schnell.
Doch meines Herrn Hand will ich führen und
    sagen:
Hier. Das ist Esau in seinem Fell.

You, my friend, are so alone,
because . . . with words and pointing fingers
slowly *we* make the world our own,
perhaps the frailest part, most full of danger.

Who points with his finger to a smell?—
But of the powers that we dread
you feel many . . . you know the dead
and are frightened by the sorcerer's spell.

Look, we together must bear alway
parcel and part, like a whole at last.
It's hard to help you. Don't plant me in

your heart—for I would grow too fast.
But I'll guide *my* master's hand and say:
Here. This is Esau in his skin.

Zu unterst der Alte, verworrn,
all der Erbauten
Wurzel, verborgener Born,
den sie nie schauten.

Sturmhelm und Jägerhorn,
Spruch von Ergrauten,
Männer im Bruderzorn,
Frauen wie Lauten . . .

Drängender Zweig an Zweig,
nirgends ein freier . . .
Einer! o steig . . . o steig . . .

Aber sie brechen noch.
Dieser erst oben doch
biegt sich zur Leier.

The first, confused, the Ancient,
the root of what's been,
the sources, concealed and latent
that's never been seen.

Helmet and hunter's horn,
graybeards' absolutes,
wrath between men born
brothers, women like lutes . . .

Branch pushing branch, on the tree
not one twig is free . . .
then one! oh, higher, higher! . . .

But they still are breaking.
The highest is taking
shape as a lyre.

Hörst du das Neue, Herr,
dröhnen und beben?
Kommen Verkündiger,
die es erheben.

Zwar ist kein Hören heil
in dem Durchtobtsein,
doch der Maschinenteil
will jetzt gelobt sein.

Sieh, die Maschine:
wie sie sich wälzt und rächt
und uns entstellt und schwächt.

Hat sie aus uns auch Kraft,
sie, ohne Leidenschaft,
treibe und diene.

Master, you hear the New,
trembling and droning?
Come now heralds who
praise it, intoning.

Really no hearing's still
hale in this turmoil,
but the machines will
have praise for toil.

See how it storms
in a rage to devour,
enervates us, deforms.

Since we gave it power,
let it run cool
and serve as a tool.

Wandelt sich rasch auch die Welt
wie Wolkengestalten,
alles Vollendete fällt
heim zum Uralten.

Über dem Wandel und Gang,
weiter und freier,
währt noch dein Vor-Gesang,
Gott mit der Leier.

Nicht sind die Leiden erkannt,
nicht ist die Liebe gelernt,
und was im Tod uns entfernt,

ist nicht entschleiert.
Einzig das Lied überm Land
heiligt und feiert.

Though the world change as fast
as cloud-shapes manifold,
all things perfected at last
fall back to the very old.

Past flux and vicissitude,
more freely and higher,
still endures your prelude,
god with the lyre.

We do not understand
grief, nor love's phases,
and what death keeps concealed

is not unveiled.
Only song through the land
hallows and praises.

Dir aber, Herr, o was weih ich dir, sag,
der das Ohr den Geschöpfen gelehrt?—
Mein Erinnern an einen Frühlingstag,
seinen Abend, in Rußland—, ein Pferd . . .

Herüber vom Dorf kam der Schimmel allein,
an der vorderen Fessel den Pflock,
um die Nacht auf den Wiesen allein zu sein;
wie schlug seiner Mähne Gelock

an den Hals im Takte des Ubermuts,
bei dem grob gehemmten Galopp.
Wie sprangen die Quellen des Rossebluts!

Der fühlte die Weiten, und ob!
der sang und der hörte—, dein Sagenkreis
war in ihm geschlossen.
   Sein Bild: ich weih's.

What shall I dedicate, Master, say,
to you who taught the creatures to hear?—
My memory of one spring day,
at evening, in Russia—a white horse there . . .

Across from the village he came alone,
a hobble on his fore fetlock,
for a night in the meadow, on his own;
on his neck tossed the shock

of his mane in time to his fiery mood,
in that clumsy gallop arrested.
What leaping fountains of stallion-blood!

He felt the spaces, oh, how great!
He neighed and listened—*in* him was invested
your saga.
His image I dedicate.

Frühling ist wiedergekommen. Die Erde
ist wie ein Kind, das Gedichte weiß;
viele, o viele . . . Für die Beschwerde
langen Lernens bekommt sie den Preis.

Streng war ihr Lehrer. Wir mochten das Weiße
an dem Barte des alten Manns.
Nun, wie das Grüne, das Blaue heiße,
dürfen wir fragen: sie kanns, sie kanns!

Erde, die frei hat, du glückliche, spiele
nun mit den Kindern. Wir wollen dich fangen,
fröhliche Erde. Dem Frohsten gelingts.

O, was der Lehrer sie lehrte, das Viele,
und was gedruckt steht in Wurzeln und langen
schwierigen Stämmen: sie singts, sie singts!

Spring has come back again. The earth
is like a child who has memorized
poems, oh, many! . . . now it seems worth
the effort, for she wins the prize.

Her teacher was strict. We loved the white
hair of the old man's beard.
When we ask what the green and the blue
   are, right
off she knows every word.

Lucky earth, with your holiday,
and all the children coming to play!
We try to catch you. The gayest will do it.

Teacher trained her until she knew it,
and all that's printed in roots and long
unruly stems she sings in a song.

Wir sind die Treibenden.
Aber den Schritt der Zeit,
nehmt ihn als Kleinigkeit
im immer Bleibenden.

Alles das Eilende
wird schon vorüber sein;
denn das Verweilende
erst weiht uns ein.

Knaben, o werft den Mut
nicht in die Schnelligkeit,
nicht in den Flugversuch.

Alles ist ausgeruht:
Dunkel und Helligkeit,
Blume und Buch.

We are the drivers.
But take time's stride
as trivial beside
what lasts forever.

The transient hastens
and soon will be over;
only what lingers
hallows and chastens.

Boys, on speed waste
no courage or power,
or on trials of flight.

Now all things rest:
darkness and light,
the book and the flower.

O erst dann, wenn der Flug
nicht mehr um seinetwillen
wird in die Himmelsstillen
steigen, sich selber genug,

um in lichten Profilen,
als das Gerät, das gelang,
Liebling der Winde zu spielen,
sicher schwenkend und schlank,—

erst wenn ein reines Wohin
wachsender Apparate
Knabenstolz überwiegt,

wird, überstürzt von Gewinn,
jener den Fernen Genahte
sein, was er einsam erfliegt.

Oh, first *when* the flight
shall no longer arise
for its own sake in the sky's
stillness, and in bright

profile, be self-sufficient,
a successful instrument,
a playful pet of the winds,
surely wheeling and slim—

not till the pure goal means
more than the growing machines
to youthful pride, will he,

by the winning overthrown,
who nears the distance *be*
what he is flying alone.

Sollen wir unsere uralte Freundschaft, die großen
niemals werbenden Götter, weil sie der harte
Stahl, den wir streng erzogen, nicht kennt,
   verstoßen
oder sie plötzlich suchen auf einer Karte?

Diese gewaltigen Freunde, die uns die Toten
nehmen, rühren nirgends an unsere Räder.
Unsere Gastmähler haben wir weit—, unsere
   Bäder,
fortgerückt, und ihre uns lang schon zu lang-
   samen Boten

überholen wir immer. Einsamer nun aufeinander
ganz angewiesen, ohne einander zu kennen,
führen wir nicht mehr die Pfade als schöne
   Mäander,

sondern als Grade. Nur noch in Dampfkesseln
   brennen
die einstigen Feuer und heben die Hämmer, die
   immer
größern. Wir aber nehmen an Kraft ab, wie
   Schwimmer.

Should we disown our oldest friendships, part
from the never-suing gods, because the hard
steel that we so rigorously have reared
does not know them? Or suddenly seek them on a
     chart?

These mighty friends, who take from us the dead,
nowhere touch our wheels. We've moved afar
our banquets and our baths; their messengers
are long too slow for us, so we have sped

past them. Now more lonely, one on another
wholly dependent, yet ignorant of each other,
we build no paths with fine meandering turns,

but by the gradient. Only in boilers burn
the former fires, lifting the hammers, ever
heavier. But we grow weak, like swimmers.

Dich aber will ich nun, dich, die ich kannte
wie eine Blume, von der ich den Namen
    nicht weiß,
noch ein Mal erinnern und ihnen zeigen,
    Entwandte,
schöne Gespielin des unüberwindlichen
    Schreis.

Tänzerin erst, die plötzlich, den Körper voll
    Zögern,
anhielt, als göß man ihr Jungsein in Erz;
trauernd und lauschend—. Da, von den
    hohen Vermögern
fiel ihr Musik in das veränderte Herz.

Nah war die Krankheit. Schon von den
    Schatten bemächtigt,
drängte verdunkelt das Blut, doch, wie
    flüchtig verdächtigt,
trieb es in seinen natürlichen Frühling hervor.

Wieder und wieder, von Dunkel und Sturz
    unterbrochen,
glänzte es irdisch. Bis es nach schrecklichem
    Pochen
trat in das trostlos offene Tor.

Once more I will remember you whom I knew
like a flower with an unknown name; yet I
will show you to them, ravished from us, you
lovely playmate of the invincible cry.

Dancer at first, then the hesitant body stood
suddenly, as if youth were cast in bronze;
sorrowing, listening. Then from the empowered
   ones
music sank into her altered blood.

Sickness drew near. Already by shadows mastered,
the darkened blood, half-suspect, could not wait,
but surged, toward its natural springtime
   bounding.

Again and again, interrupted by dark and
   disaster,
it glittered, earthly. Till after terrible pounding
it entered the desolate open gate.

Du aber, Göttlicher, du, bis zuletzt noch Ertöner,
da ihn der Schwarm der verschmähten Mänaden
befiel,
hast ihr Geschrei übertönt mit Ordnung, du
Schöner,
aus den Zerstörenden stieg dein erbauendes Spiel.

Keine war da, daß sie Haupt dir und Leier
zerstör',
wie sie auch rangen und rasten; und alle die
scharfen
Steine, die sie nach deinem Herzen warfen,
wurden zu Sanftem an dir und begabt mit
Gehör.

Schließlich zerschlugen sie dich, von der Rache
gehetzt,
während dein Klang noch in Löwen und Felsen
verweilte
und in den Bäumen und Vögeln. Dort singst du
noch jetzt.

O du verlorener Gott! Du unendliche Spur!
Nur weil dich reißend zuletzt die Feindschaft
verteilte,
sind wir die Hörenden jetzt und ein Mund der
Natur.

But you, divine one, unto the last still singing,
although attacked by the flouted Maenads'
throng,
beautiful god, above the shrieks rose ringing
among the destroyers your ordered upbuilding
song.

There was none there could harm your head or
harp,
however they raved and struggled; all the sharp

stones they cast at you grew soft when nearing
your heart and, touching you, were endowed with
hearing.

Finally, driven by vengeance, they broke and tore
your body, but in cliffs and lions lingered
your music, in birds and trees. You still sing there.

O you lost god! You never-ending clue!
Only since hatred at last parceled you
among us, are we hearers and a mouth for nature.

Atmen, du unsichtbares Gedicht!
Immerfort um das eigne
Sein rein eingetauschter Weltraum.
   Gegengewicht,
in dem ich mich rhythmisch ereigne.

Einzige Welle, deren
allmähliches Meer ich bin;
sparsamstes du von allen möglichen
   Meeren,—
Raumgewinn.

Wie viele von diesen Stellen der
   Räume waren schon
innen in mir. Manche Winde
sind wie mein Sohn.

Erkennst du mich, Luft, du, voll noch
   einst meiniger Orte?
Du, einmal glatte Rinde,
Rundung und Blatt meiner Worte.

1

Breath, you invisible poem! Pure
exchange unceasing between the great
ether and our existence. Counterweight
in which I rhythmically occur.

Single billow whose slow degrees
of ocean take place
in me; most frugal, you, of all possible seas—
winnings of space.

How many parts of this space already were
within me! There's many a wind
like a son to me.

Do you know me, air, full of places where I
   used to be?
You, once smooth rind,
roundness and leaf of my words.

2

So wie dem Meister manchmal das eilig
nähere Blatt den wirklichen Strich
abnimmt: so nehmen oft Spiegel das heilig
einzige Lächeln der Mädchen in sich,

wenn sie den Morgen erproben, allein,—
oder im Glanze der dienenden Lichter.
Und in das Atmen der echten Gesichter,
später, fällt nur ein Widerschein.

Was haben Augen einst ins umrußte
lange Verglühn der Kamine geschaut:
Blicke des Lebens, für immer verlorne.

Ach, der Erde, wer kennt die Verluste?
Nur, wer mit dennoch preisendem Laut
sänge das Herz, das ins Ganze geborne.

2

Even as a handy sheet of paper
sometimes catches a *genuine* master-stroke,
so, often into themselves the mirrors
take the one blessèd smile of girls who awoke

and tried out the morning, alone—
or in the attendant lights' glitter.
And where the breath of their real faces
　shone
there falls but a mere reflection, later.

What have eyes once seen in the blackening
　coals
slowly cooling upon the hearth?
Glimpses of life, forever lost.

Ah, who knows the losses of earth?
Only one, who praises nevertheless,
can sing the heart born into the Whole.

Spiegel: noch nie hat man wissend beschrieben,
was ihr in euerem Wesen seid.
Ihr, wie mit lauter Löchern von Sieben
erfüllten Zwischenräume der Zeit.

Ihr, noch des leeren Saales Verschwender—,
wenn es dämmert, wie Wälder weit . . .
Und der Lüster geht wie ein Sechzehn-Ender
durch eure Unbetretbarkeit.

Manchmal seid ihr voll Malerei.
Einige scheinen in euch gegangen—,
andere schicktet ihr scheu vorbei.

Aber die Schönste wird bleiben, bis
drüben in ihre enthaltenen Wangen
eindrang der klare gelöste Narziß.

Mirrors: still no one knowing has told
what your essential nature is.
You, entirely filled, as with holes
of sieves, you, time's interstices.

You, wastrels still of the empty hall—
broad as the woods, when the twilight falls . . .
and the chandelier, like a sixteen-pointer,
pierces you none else can enter.

Often you are full of paintings. A few
seem to have passed straight into you;
others you timidly sent past.

But the loveliest one will stay, till there
to her withheld cheeks the unbounded clear
Narcissus forces his way at last.

O dieses ist das Tier, das es nicht gibt.
Sie wußtens nicht und habens jeden Falls
—sein Wandeln, seine Haltung, seinen Hals,
bis in des stillen Blickes Licht—geliebt.

Zwar war es nicht. Doch weil sie's liebten, ward
ein reines Tier. Sie ließen immer Raum.
Und in dem Raume, klar und ausgespart,
erhob es leicht sein Haupt und brauchte kaum

zu sein. Sie nährten es mit keinem Korn,
nur immer mit der Möglichkeit, es sei.
Und die gab solche Stärke an das Tier,

daß es aus sich ein Stirnhorn trieb. Ein Horn.
Zu einer Jungfrau kam es weiß herbei—
und war im Silber-Spiegel und in ihr.

Oh, this is the animal that never was.
They did not know it and, for all of that,
they loved his neck and posture, and his gait,
clean to the great eyes with their tranquil gaze.

Really it *was* not. Of their love they made it,
this pure creature. And they left a space
always, till in this clear uncluttered place
lightly he raised his head and scarcely needed

to be. They did not feed him any corn,
only the possibility he might
exist, which gave the beast such strength, he bore

a horn upon the forehead. Just one horn.
Unto a virgin he appeared, all white,
and was in the silver mirror and in her.

Blumenmuskel, der der Anemone
Wiesenmorgen nach und nach erschließt,
bis in ihren Schooß das polyphone
Licht der lauten Himmel sich ergießt,

in den stillen Blütenstern gespannter
Muskel des unendlichen Empfangs,
manchmal so von Fülle übermannter,
daß der Ruhewink des Untergangs

kaum vermag die weitzurückgeschnellten
Blätterränder dir zurückzugeben:
du, Entschluß und Kraft von wieviel Welten!

Wir Gewaltsamen, wir währen länger.
Aber wann, in welchem aller Leben,
sind wir endlich offen und Empfänger?

Flower-muscle of the anemone
that little by little opens to the meadow-dawn,
until light's mighty polyphone pours down
into the womb from the sonorous sky,

muscle of infinite receptivity
so tautened in the still star of the bloom,
often with *such* abundance overcome
that the sunset's beckoning peacefully

is barely strong enough again to give
the far-sprung petal rims to you: O power
and resolution of *how many* worlds!

We, the violent, though we endure
longer, *when,* in which of all our lives
are we receivers finally unfurled?

Rose, du thronende, denen im Altertume
warst du ein Kelch mit einfachem Rand.
Uns aber bist du die volle zahllose Blume,
der unerschöpfliche Gebenstand.

In deinem Reichtum scheinst du wie
    Kleidung um Kleidung
um einen Leib aus nichts als Glanz;
aber dein einzelnes Blatt ist zugleich die
    Vermeidung
und die Verleugnung jedes Gewands.

Seit Jahrhunderten ruft uns dein Duft
seine süßesten Namen herüber;
plötzlich liegt er wie Ruhm in der Luft.

Dennoch, wir wissen ihn nicht zu nennen,
    wir raten . . .
Und Erinnerung geht zu ihm über,
die wir von rufbaren Stunden erbaten.

Roses, you on a throne, in antiquity
were a calyx in a simple ring.
But to *us* you're the full flower, an innumerably
inexhaustible thing.

In your richness you shine, with garment on
     garment
on a body of nothing but radiance;
yet a single petal is at once the avoidance
and denial of any raiment.

Your fragrance calls its sweetest names
across the centuries to us;
suddenly it lies plain in the air as fame.

But we do not know what to name it, we
     guess . . .
and memory surrenders to it all
that we have begged from hours evocable.

Blumen, ihr schließlich den ordnenden Händen
  verwandte,
(Händen der Mädchen von einst und jetzt),
die auf dem Gartentisch oft von Kante zu Kante
lagen, ermattet und sanft verletzt,

wartend des Wassers, das sie noch einmal erhole
aus dem begonnenen Tod—, und nun
wieder erhobene zwischen die strömenden Pole
fühlender Finger, die wohlzutun

mehr noch vermögen, als ihr ahntet, ihr leichten,
wenn ihr euch wiederfandet im Krug,
langsam erkühlend und Warmes der Mädchen,
  wie Beichten,

von euch gebend, wie trübe ermüdende Sünden,
die das Gepflücktsein beging, als Bezug
wieder zu ihnen, die sich euch blühend verbünden.

Flowers, finally to ordering hands related
(hands of girls of long ago and today),
who often across the garden table lay,
meekly wounded and wilted,

awaiting the water to make you recover
from the death begun—now raised anew
between the dripping poles of tender
fingers that can do,

light ones, even better than you guessed,
when you came to in the vase, and cooling
slowly gave out the warmth of girls, like confessed

sins, how wearisome and gloomy,
committed by being picked, a bond made newly
with them who are your confederates in blooming.

Wenige ihr, der einstigen Kindheit Gespielen
in den zerstreuten Gärten der Stadt:
wie wir uns fanden und uns zögernd gefielen
und, wie das Lamm mit dem redenden Blatt,

sprachen als schweigende. Wenn wir uns einmal
   freuten,
keinem gehörte es. Wessen wars?
Und wie zergings unter allen den gehenden Leuten
und im Bangen des langen Jahrs.

Wagen umrollten uns fremd, vorübergezogen,
Häuser umstanden uns stark, aber unwahr,—und
   keines
kannte uns je. Was war wirklich im All?

Nichts. Nur die Bälle. Ihre herrlichen Bogen.
Auch nicht die Kinder . . . Aber manchmal trat
   eines,
ach ein vergehendes, unter den fallenden Ball.

In memoriam Egon von Rilke

You few playmates of childhood long ago
in scattered city gardens: how we found
each other and grew hesitantly fond
and, like the lamb with the speaking scroll,
  although

speaking, were silent. All our fun belonged
to no one. Whose could it be?
And how it dissolved wherever people thronged,
and under the long year's anxiety!

Carriages passed us, strangers. Solid, dark,
houses stood near, make-believe—and none
knew us ever. *What* was real in the All?

Nothing. Except the balls. Their splendid arcs.
Not even the children . . . but sometimes there
  was one,
ah, dying, who walked under the falling ball.

In memoriam Egon von Rilke

Rühmt euch, ihr Richtenden, nicht der
entbehrlichen Folter
und daß das Eisen nicht länger an Hälsen
sperrt.
Keins ist gesteigert, kein Herz—, weil ein
gewollter
Krampf der Milde euch zarter verzerrt.

Was es durch Zeiten bekam, das schenkt das
Schafott
wieder zurück, wie Kinder ihr Spielzeug vom
vorig
alten Geburtstag. Ins reine, ins hohe, ins
torig
offene Herz träte er anders, der Gott

wirklicher Milde. Er käme gewaltig und griffe
strahlender um sich, wie Göttliche sind.
Mehr als ein Wind für die großen gesicher-
ten Schiffe.

Weniger nicht, als die heimliche leise
Gewahrung,
die uns im Innern schweigend gewinnt
wie ein still spielendes Kind aus unendlicher
Paarung.

Do not boast, you judges, of irons not clamped
on necks, or of the spared rack and thumbscrew.
No heart is lifted, none—since the purposed
  cramp
of mercy is more gently twisting you.

What it's had from time the scaffold gives back
  again,
as children the toys from birthdays of last year.
Into the lofty, gate-like heart, the pure
and open heart, how different he'd enter then,

the god of true mercy. Violently come and grip
with radiance round him, like the gods, his kin.
More than a wind for the confident great ships.

Not less than the gentle secret perception
that overcomes us silently within,
like a quietly playing child of an infinite concep-
  tion.

Alles Erworbne bedroht die Maschine, solange
sie sich erdreistet, im Geist, statt im Gehorchen,
zu sein.
Daß nicht der herrlichen Hand schöneres Zögern
mehr prange,
zu dem entschlossenern Bau schneidet sie steifer
den Stein.

Nirgends bleibt sie zurück, daß wir ihr ein Mal
entrönnen
und sie in stiller Fabrik ölend sich selber gehört.
Sie ist das Leben,—sie meint es am besten zu
können,
die mit dem gleichen Entschluß ordnet und
schafft und zerstört.

Aber noch ist uns das Dasein verzaubert; an
hundert
Stellen ist es noch Ursprung. Ein Spielen von
reinen
Kräften, die keiner berührt, der nicht kniet und
bewundert.

Worte gehen noch zart am Unsäglichen aus . . .
Und die Musik, immer neu, aus den bebendsten
Steinen,
baut im unbrauchbaren Raum ihr vergöttlichtes
Haus.

All we have won is threatened by the machine,
  so long
as it, instead of obeying, as spirit dares to
  command.
For the more resolute building it cuts more stiffly
  the stone,
lest it shine from the fairer lingering of the
  master-hand.

Nowhere stands the machine aside, that we
  escape *once*,
where it oils and belongs to itself in the factory
  without noise.
It is life—and it believes in its omniscience,
as with like resolution it orders and makes and
  destroys.

But still for us existence is enchanted: from a
  hundred places
it is still origin. A play of pure forces
that no one touches unless he kneels and admires.

The Unutterable, words fragilely slip by . . .
and from the most vibrant stones music anew
  aspires
building her deified house in the useless space
  of the sky.

Manche, des Todes, entstand ruhig geordnete
   Regel,
weiterbezwingender Mensch, seit du im Jagen
   beharrst;
mehr doch als Falle und Netz, weiß ich dich,
   Streifen von Segel,
den man hinuntergehängt in den höhligen Karst.

Leise ließ man dich ein, als wärst du ein Zeichen,
Frieden zu feiern. Doch dann: rang dich am
   Rande der Knecht,
—und, aus den Höhlen, die Nacht warf eine
   Handvoll von bleichen
taumelnden Tauben ins Licht . . .
      Aber auch das ist im Recht.

Fern von dem Schauenden sei jeglicher Hauch
   des Bedauerns,
nicht nur vom Jäger allein, der, was sich zeitig
   erweist,
wachsam und handelnd vollzieht.

Töten ist eine Gestalt unseres wandernden
   Trauerns . . .
Rein ist im heiteren Geist,
was an uns selber geschieht.

Many a quietly ordered rule of death now
  prevails,
onpressing, conquering man, since you undertook
  hunting first;
but better than trap and net, I know you, strip
  of sail,
that they let down into the caverns of Karst.

Gently they slipped you in, as if you were a
  pledge
to celebrate peace. But then, the fellow twisted
  your edge—
and a handful of white and reeling doves was
  thrown by the night
from the caverns into the day . . .
            but even *that* has its right.

Afar from the spectators be every breath of
  compassion,
not only from the hunter, who vigilantly takes
  heed
and effects the timely deed.

*Killing is only an aspect of the wandering grief
  we endure . . .*
To the spirit without passion
what happens to us is pure.

Wolle die Wandlung. O sei für die Flamme
    begeistert,
drin sich ein Ding dir entzieht, das mit
    Verwandlungen prunkt;
jener entwerfende Geist, welcher das Irdische
    meistert,
liebt in dem Schwung der Figur nichts wie den
    wendenden Punkt.

Was sich ins Bleiben verschließt, schon ists das
    Erstarrte;
wähnt es sich sicher im Schutz des unscheinbaren
    Grau's?
Warte, ein Härtestes warnt aus der Ferne das
    Harte.
Wehe—: abwesender Hammer holt aus!

Wer sich als Quelle ergießt, den erkennt die
    Erkennung;
und sie führt ihn entzückt durch das heiter
    Geschaffne,
das mit Anfang oft schließt und mit Ende
    beginnt.

Jeder glückliche Raum ist Kind oder Enkel von
    Trennung,
den sie staunend durchgehn. Und die verwandelte
    Daphne
will, seit sie lorbeern fühlt, daß du dich wandelst
    in Wind.

Will the transformation. Oh, be inspired by the
 burning
flame in which something that boasts of
 transformation withdraws;
that scheme-devising spirit, which masters earthly
 laws,
loves nothing so much in the soaring of symbols
 as the point of turning.

What shuts itself in abiding *is* already numb. It
 believes
itself safe in the shelter of unostentatious gray?
Wait, a hardest forewarns the hard from far
 away.
Alas, an absent hammer upheaves!

He who pours out himself as a spring is
 perceived by Perceiving,
that conducts him enraptured through all the
 cheerful creation,
which often ends at the start and begins at the
 end.

Every happy space is a child or grandchild of
 Leaving,
in which they wander astounded. And Daphne,
 since transformation,
feeling herself laurel, wills that you change to
 a wind.

Sei allem Abschied voran, als wäre er hinter
dir, wie der Winter, der eben geht.
Denn unter Wintern ist einer so endlos Winter,
daß, überwinternd, dein Herz überhaupt
übersteht.

Sei immer tot in Eurydike—, singender steige,
preisender steige zurück in den reinen Bezug.
Hier, unter Schwindenden, sei, im Reiche der
Neige,
sei ein klingendes Glas, das sich im Klang schon
zerschlug.

Sei—und wisse zugleich des Nicht-Seins
Bedingung,
den unendlichen Grund deiner innigen
Schwingung,
daß du sie völlig vollziehst dieses einzige Mal.

Zu dem gebrauchten sowohl, wie zum dumpfen
und stummen
Vorrat der vollen Natur, den unsäglichen
Summen,
zähle dich jubelnd hinzu und vernichte die Zahl.

Keep ahead of all parting, as if it were behind
you, like the winter that is just now passed.
In winters you are so endlessly winter, you find
that, getting through winter, your heart on the
    whole will last.

Be ever dead in Eurydice—arise singing
with greater praise, rise again to the pure relation.
Among the fleeting, in the realm of declination,
be a resonant glass that shatters while it is
    ringing.

Be—at the same time, know the terms of
    negation,
the infinite basis of your fervent vibration,
that you may completely complete it this one
    time.

To teeming nature's store of used, as of dumb
and moldy things, to that uncountable count,
add yourself joyously, and annul the amount.

Siehe die Blumen, diese dem Irdischen treuen,
denen wir Schicksal vom Rande des Schicksals
    leihn,—
aber wer weiß es! Wenn sie ihr Welken bereuen,
ist es an uns, ihre Reue zu sein.

Alles will schweben. Da gehn wir umher wie Be-
    schwerer,
legen auf alles uns selbst, vom Gewichte entzückt;
o was sind wir den Dingen für zehrende Lehrer,
weil ihnen ewige Kindheit glückt.

Nähme sie einer ins innige Schlafen und schliefe
tief mit den Dingen—: o wie käme er leicht,
anders zum anderen Tag, aus der gemeinsamen
    Tiefe.

Oder er bliebe vielleicht; und sie blühten und
    priesen
ihn, den Bekehrten, der nun den Ihrigen gleicht,
allen den stillen Geschwistern im Winde der
    Wiesen.

14

Look at the flowers, faithful to earth's ways,
to whom we lend fate from fate's very rim—
but who knows? If they grieve that they decay,
we must be the grief for them.

All wills to float, yet heavily here and there,
we lie on everything, glad of our weight;
what consuming teachers we are for the Things
     to bear,
that are happy in their ever-childish state.

If one took them into intimate sleep and slept
deeply with the Things, ah, how light he
     would grow!
changed in a new day, out of the common
     depth.

Or maybe he would stay; and they'd flower
     and acclaim
him, the converted, who would then be like
     them,
all the still brothers and sisters where meadow-
     winds blow.

O Brunnen-Mund, du gebender, du Mund,
der unerschöpflich Eines, Reines, spricht,—
du, vor des Wassers fließendem Gesicht,
marmorne Maske. Und im Hintergrund

der Aquädukte Herkunft. Weither an
Gräbern vorbei, vom Hang des Apennins
tragen sie dir dein Sagen zu, das dann
am schwarzen Altern deines Kinns

vorüberfällt in das Gefäß davor.
Dies ist das schlafend hingelegte Ohr,
das Marmor-Ohr, in das du immer sprichst.

Ein Ohr der Erde. Nur mit sich allein
redet sie also. Schiebt ein Krug sich ein,
so scheint es ihr, daß du sie unterbrichst.

O fountain-mouth, you giver, O you round
mouth speaking inexhaustibly one pure
thing, you mask of marble placed before
the flowing face of water. The background

is marching aqueducts. From far away,
passing the tombs, from the slope of the
  Apennines,
they carry to you what you are going to say,
which beyond the black ageing of your chin

falls into the basin there below.
This is the ear laid down, asleep,
the ear of marble into which you speak

forever. An ear of earth. She talks alone
to herself, and when sometimes a pitcher's slipped
under the flow, she thinks you interrupt.

Immer wieder von uns aufgerissen,
ist der Gott die Stelle, welche heilt.
Wir sind Scharfe, denn wir wollen wissen,
aber er ist heiter und verteilt.

Selbst die reine, die geweihte Spende
nimmt er anders nicht in seine Welt,
als indem er sich dem freien Ende
unbewegt entgegenstellt.

Nur der Tote trinkt
aus der hier von uns gehörten Quelle,
wenn der Gott ihm schweigend winkt,
    dem Toten.

Uns wird nur das Lärmen angeboten.
Und das Lamm erbittet seine Schelle
aus dem stilleren Instinkt.

Always torn open by us again,
the god is the place that heals.
We are Sharpness, because we will
to know; he's divided and serene.

Even the pure, the avowed donation
he accepts in his world in so far as he
opposes himself to the free
end, without motion.

We *hear* the flowing from that well
where none but the dead drink,
when the god beckons them silently, the dead.

Only its hubbub's offered *us* instead.
And with a more quiet instinct
the lamb begs for his bell.

Wo, in welchen immer selig bewässerten Gärten,
   an welchen
Bäumen, aus welchen zärtlich entblätterten
   Blüten-Kelchen
reifen die fremdartigen Früchte der Tröstung?
   Diese
köstlichen, deren du eine vielleicht in der zer-
   tretenen Wiese

deiner Armut findest. Von einem zum anderen
   Male
wunderst du dich über die Größe der Frucht,
über ihr Heilsein, über die Sanftheit der Schale,
und daß sie der Leichtsinn des Vogels dir nicht
   vorwegnahm und nicht die Eifersucht

unten des Wurms. Gibt es denn Bäume, von
   Engeln beflogen,
und von verborgenen langsamen Gärtnern so
   seltsam gezogen,
daß sie uns tragen, ohne uns zu gehören?

Haben wir niemals vermocht, wir Schatten und
   Schemen,
durch unser voreilig reifes und wieder welkes
   Benehmen
jener gelassenen Sommer Gleichmut zu
   stören?

17

Where, in what ever-happily watered garden,
   on what trees,
from what tenderly stripped flower-calices
ripen the strange fruits of consolation? Those
   delicate fruits
of which you perhaps find one underfoot

in the trodden field of your poverty. Time
   after time,
you're amazed at the size of the fruit, at the
   tenderness
of its skin, at its wholesomeness,
and that the carelessness of a bird or envious
   worm

has not forestalled you. *Are* there trees,
   thronged by angels,
by slow and secret gardeners tended so
   strangely,
that they bear for us, without our being the
   owners?

Have we never been able, we phantoms and
   shades,
by our actions, too early ripened and soon to
   fade,
to disturb the serenity of these imperturbable
   summers?

Tänzerin: o du Verlegung
alles Vergehens in Gang: wie brachtest du's
dar.
Und der Wirbel am Schluß, dieser Baum aus
Bewegung,
nahm er nicht ganz in Besitz das erschwungene
Jahr?

Blühte nicht, daß ihn dein Schwingen von
vorhin umschwärme,
plötzlich sein Wipfel von Stille? Und über ihr,
war sie nicht Sonne, war sie nicht Sommer,
die Wärme,
diese unzählige Wärme aus dir?

Aber er trug auch, er trug, dein Baum der
Ekstase.
Sind sie nicht seine ruhigen Früchte: der Krug,
reifend gestreift, und die gereiftere Vase?

Und in den Bildern: ist nicht die Zeichnung
geblieben,
die deiner Braue dunkler Zug
rasch an die Wandung der eigenen Wendung
geschrieben?

Dancer: O you translation
of all transiency into action, how you made it
  clear!
And the whirl of the finish, that tree of motion,
didn't it wholly take in the hard-won year?

And didn't its summit, so that your flourish just
  now could swarm
about it, blossom with stillness? And up in the
  blue
wasn't it summer and sunlight, with the warm
immeasurable warmth from you?

But it also bore, it bore, your tree of rapture.
Aren't these its peaceful fruits: the pitcher
striped with ripening, and the more ripened
  vase?

And in the decoration: has not the drawing
endured, the dark line your eyebrows traced
swiftly in the texture of their own turning?

Irgendwo wohnt das Gold in der verwöhnenden
    Bank,
und mit Tausenden tut es vertraulich. Doch jener
Blinde, der Bettler, ist selbst dem kupfernen
    Zehner
wie ein verlorener Ort, wie das staubige Eck
    unterm Schrank.

In den Geschäften entlang ist das Geld wie zu
    Hause
und verkleidet sich scheinbar in Seide, Nelken und
    Pelz.
Er, der Schweigende, steht in der Atempause
alles des wach oder schlafend atmenden Gelds.

O wie mag sie sich schließen bei Nacht, diese
    immer offene Hand.
Morgen holt sie das Schicksal wieder, und täglich
hält es sie hin: hell, elend, unendlich zerstörbar.

Daß doch einer, ein Schauender, enlich ihren
    langen Bestand
staunend begriffe und rühmte. Nur dem Auf-
    singenden säglich.
Nur dem Göttlichen hörbar.

Somewhere lives gold in the indulgent bank,
on familiar terms with thousands. Nevertheless,
that blindman, the beggar, to a penny's like
a lost place, a dusty corner behind the clothes-
press.

Money feels quite at home in all the shops,
plausibly dressed in silk, with carnations and furs.
But the silent beggar waits in all the stops
between the breaths of all money that sleeps or
stirs.

Oh, how can it close at night, that ever-open
hand?
Tomorrow fate brings it again, holds it out every
day:
miserable, infinitely destructible, clear.

If but some clairvoyant could at last understand
astonished, and praise its duration, as only a
singer may!
For only a god to hear.

Zwischen den Sternen, wie weit; und doch, um
    wievieles noch weiter,
was man am Hiesigen lernt.
Einer, zum Beispiel, ein Kind . . . und ein
    Nächster, ein Zweiter—,
o wie unfaßlich entfernt.

Schicksal, es mißt uns vielleicht mit des Seienden
    Spanne,
daß es uns fremd erscheint;
denk, wieviel Spannen allein vom Mädchen zum
    Manne,
wenn es ihn meidet und meint.

Alles ist weit—, und nirgends schließt sich der
    Kreis.
Sieh in der Schüssel, auf heiter bereitetem Tische,
seltsam der Fische Gesicht.

Fische sind stumm . . . , meinte man einmal. Wer
    weiß?
Aber ist nicht am Ende ein Ort, wo man das, was
    der Fische
Sprache wäre, ohne sie spricht?

Between the stars, how far, and still much farther
is what one learns by existence.
Someone, for instance, a child . . . a neighbor . . .
  another—
oh, how inconceivably distant.

Maybe destiny measures us with spans of being,
and thus seems inauspicious;
but think, how many spans between the girl
  fleeing
and the man whom she wishes.

Everything is remote—and nowhere does the circle
  close.
On the cheerfully set table, see in the dish
how odd are the faces of fish.

Fish are mute . . . one used to think. Who knows?
But is there no place at last where, from each to
  each
there is something that might be language,
  without speech?

Singe die Gärten, mein Herz, die du nicht kennst;
   wie in Glas
eingegossene Gärten, klar, unerreichbar.
Wasser und Rosen von Ispahan oder Schiras,
singe sie selig, preise sie, keinem vergleichbar.

Zeige, mein Herz, daß du sie niemals entbehrst.
Daß sie dich meinen, ihre reifenden Feigen.
Daß du mit ihren, zwischen den blühenden
   Zweigen
wie zum Gesicht gesteigerten Lüften verkehrst.

Meide den Irrtum, daß es Entbehrungen gebe
für den geschehnen Entschluß, diesen: zu sein!
Seidener Faden, kamst du hinein ins Gewebe.

Welchem der Bilder du auch im Innern geeint
   bist
(sei es selbst ein Moment aus dem Leben der
   Pein),
fühl, daß der ganze, der rühmliche Teppich
   gemeint ist.

Sing, my heart, the unknown gardens poured
crystalline, inaccessible, as in glass.
Sing their rapture, praise them as compared
to none, those waters and roses of Shiraz

or Ispahan. My heart, show you never miss them.
That their ripening figs intend themselves for you.
That you are the friend of breezes blowing through
the flowering boughs, increasing as if to visions.

Avoid the mistake of thinking privation's caused
by a resolution taken, that is: to be!
Silken thread, you were woven in the frame.

No matter what pattern you feel most inwardly
(though it be a moment from the life of pain),
remember, a whole grand carpet is proposed.

O trotz Schicksal: die herrlichen Überflüsse
unseres Daseins, in Parken übergeschäumt,—
oder als steinerne Männer neben die Schlüsse
hoher Portale, unter Balkone gebäumt!

O die eherne Glocke, die ihre Keule
täglich wider den stumpfen Alltag hebt.
Oder die eine, in Karnak, die Säule, die
    Säule,
die fast ewige Tempel überlebt.

Heute stürzen die Überschüsse, dieselben,
nur noch als Eile vorbei, aus dem wagrechten
    gelben
Tag in die blendend mit Licht übertriebene
    Nacht.

Aber das Rasen zergeht und läßt keine Spuren.
Kurven des Flugs durch die Luft und die, die
    sie fuhren,
keine vielleicht ist umsonst. Doch nur wie
    gedacht.

Oh, the splendid overflow, in spite of fate,
of our existence. In the parks, foaming, out-
  poured—
or as stone figures, under the balconies reared,
beside the keystones of the lofty gates!

Oh, the brazen bell each day upheaving
against the banal everyday its cudgel.
Or the *one*, the column, the column outliving
in Karnak the almost eternal temple.

Today the same surpluses rush past, but as naught
save speed, from the yellow horizontal day
into the light-bedazzled immoderate night.

But, leaving no trace, the delirium fades away.
The curves through the air and those who guided
  the flight,
none is in vain perhaps. But just as if thought.

Rufe mich zu jener deiner Stunden,
die dir unaufhörlich widersteht:
flehend nah wie das Gesicht von Hunden,
aber immer wieder weggedreht,

wenn du meinst, sie endlich zu erfassen.
So Entzognes ist am meisten dein.
Wir sind frei. Wir wurden dort entlassen,
wo wir meinten, erst begrüßt zu sein.

Bang verlangen wir nach einem Halte,
wir zu Jungen manchmal für das Alte
und zu alt für das, was niemals war.

Wir, gerecht nur, wo wir dennoch preisen,
weil wir, ach, der Ast sind und das Eisen
und das Süße reifender Gefahr.

Call me to one of your hours, the space
that always opposes you:
suppliant, close as a dog's face,
but always turning away anew

when you believe it's finally caught.
That is most yours which is thus withdrawn.
We are free, for where we thought
to have been welcomed, we were sent on.

Anxiously we crave a hold,
we, too young often for what is old
and too old for what never happened.

We are just but to what we praise anyhow,
for, ah, we are the iron and the bough
and the sweetness of danger that ripens.

O diese Lust, immer neu, aus gelockertem Lehm!
Niemand beinah hat den frühesten Wagern
   geholfen.
Städte entstanden trotzdem an beseligten Golfen,
Wasser und Öl füllten die Krüge trotzdem.

Götter, wir planen sie erst in erkühnten Ent-
   würfen,
die uns das mürrische Schicksal wieder zerstört.
Aber sie sind die Unsterblichen. Sehet, wir dürfen
jenen erhorchen, der uns am Ende erhört.

Wir, ein Geschlecht durch Jahrtausende: Mütter
   und Väter,
immer erfüllter von dem künftigen Kind,
daß es uns einst, übersteigend, erschüttere, später.

Wir, wir unendlich Gewagten, was haben wir
   Zeit!
Und nur der schweigsame Tod, der weiß, was wir
   sind
und was er immer gewinnt, wenn er uns leiht.

Oh, this pleasure, always new, from the loosened
   clay!
Almost no one helped in the earliest ventures.
But, despite that, cities rose by happy bays;
in spite of it, oil and water filled the pitchers.

The gods, we project them first with hardihood,
and surly destiny destroys them again.
But they are the deathless ones. Look here, we
   should
hear him through who will hear us in the end.

We, a race through thousands of years: fathers
and mothers, ever more full of the future birth,
which, one day surpassing us, will shatter us, later.

We, we the endlessly risked, what aeons we own!
And only Death, the laconic, knows what we're
   worth
and how much he always gains when he puts us
   on loan.

Schon, horch, hörst du der ersten Harken
Arbeit; wieder den menschlichen Takt
in der verhaltenen Stille der starken
Vorfrühlingserde. Unabgeschmackt

scheint dir das Kommende. Jenes so oft
dir schon Gekommene scheint dir zu kommen
wieder wie Neues. Immer erhofft,
nahmst du es niemals. Es hat dich genommen.

Selbst die Blätter durchwinterter Eichen
scheinen im Abend ein künftiges Braun.
Manchmal geben sich Lüfte ein Zeichen.

Schwarz sind die Sträucher. Doch Haufen von
    Dünger
lagern als satteres Schwarz in den Au'n.
Jede Stunde, die hingeht, wird jünger.

Already, listen, you hear the first harrows
at work: again man's rhythms teem
in the tense stillness of tomorrow's
strong spring earth. What is coming seems

insipid no longer. Not the same
as that last year, but as something new.
Always expected, but when it came,
you never got it. It got you.

Even by the leaves of the wintered oaks
at evening a future brown's revealed.
Often the breezes exchange tokens.

Black are the bushes, but piles of dung
of a richer black lie on the fields.
Each passing hour grows more young.

Wie ergreift uns der Vogelschrei . . .
Irgendein einmal erschaffenes Schreien.
Aber die Kinder schon, spielend im Freien,
schreien an wirklichen Schreien vorbei.

Schreien den Zufall. In Zwischenräume
dieses, des Weltraums, (in welchen der heile
Vogelschrei eingeht, wie Menschen in Träume—)
treiben sie ihre, des Kreischens, Keile.

Wehe, wo sind wir? Immer noch freier,
wie die losgerissenen Drachen
jagen wir halbhoch, mit Rändern von Lachen,

windig zerfetzten.—Ordne die Schreier,
singender Gott! daß sie rauschend erwachen,
tragend als Strömung das Haupt und die Leier.

We are stirred by a bird's cry . . .
any once-created crying.
But outside, the children playing
cry beyond actual cries.

Cry the hazard. Into the spaces
of ether (where the bird's cry passes
unscathed, like men in dreams),
they drive the wedges of their screams.

Alas, where are we? Ever more free,
like loose kites, with edges of laughter,
we race through mid-air, wind-tattered.

—Singing god! set in order these criers,
so they may awaken roaringly,
as a river bearing the head and the lyre.

Gibt es wirklich die Zeit, die zerstörende?
Wann, auf dem ruhenden Berg, zerbricht sie die
  Burg?
Dieses Herz, das unendlich den Göttern ge-
  hörende,
wann vergewaltigts der Demiurg?

Sind wir wirklich so ängstlich Zerbrechliche,
wie das Schicksal uns wahrmachen will?
Ist die Kindheit, die tiefe, versprechliche,
in den Wurzeln—später—still?

Ach, das Gespenst des Vergänglichen,
durch den arglos Empfänglichen
geht es, als wär es ein Rauch.

Als die, die wir sind, als die Treibenden,
gelten wir doch bei bleibenden
Kräften als göttlicher Brauch.

Does it really exist, this destroyer, Time?
When will it break the castle to shards
on the calm mountain? And the demiurge tame
this heart that forever belongs to the gods?

Are we really so fearfully fragile
as fate would prove to us?
Is childhood, deep and full of promise,
in the roots—later—tranquil?

Ah, the specter of the transient,
like a smoke-wraith, passes
through the guileless receiver.

As what we are, as drivers,
we count among permanent
powers for divine uses.

O komm und geh. Du, fast noch Kind, ergänze
für einen Augenblick die Tanzfigur
zum reinen Sternbild eines jener Tänze,
darin wir die dumpf ordnende Natur

vergänglich übertreffen. Denn sie regte
sich völlig hörend nur, da Orpheus sang.
Du warst noch die von damals her Bewegte
und leicht befremdet, wenn ein Baum sich lang

besann, mit dir nach dem Gehör zu gehn.
Du wußtest noch die Stelle, wo die Leier
sich tönend hob—; die unerhörte Mitte.

Für sie versuchtest du die schönen Schritte
und hofftest, einmal zu der heilen Feier
des Freundes Gang und Antlitz hinzudrehn.

Oh, come and go. You, almost a child, complete
for an instant the dance-figure, that it be
a pure constellation by which we beat
the order of stupid nature transiently.

Yes, for it was nature that first stirred
fully just to listen to Orpheus' song.
You were excited from the time you heard
and felt it strange when any tree thought long

whether it would go with you by ear.
You still knew where the lyre was raised to call,
resounding—the unheard-of center. Therefore,

you tried the lovely steps and hoped to turn
the eyes and footsteps of your friend to learn
for once the whole and healing festival.

Stiller Freund der vielen Fernen, fühle,
wie dein Atem noch den Raum vermehrt.
Im Gebälk der finstern Glockenstühle
laß dich läuten. Das, was an dir zehrt,

wird ein Starkes über dieser Nahrung.
Geh in der Verwandlung aus und ein.
Was ist deine leidendste Erfahrung?
Ist dir Trinken bitter, werde Wein.

Sei in dieser Nacht aus Übermaß
Zauberkraft am Kreuzweg deiner Sinne,
ihrer seltsamen Begegnung Sinn.

Und wenn dich das Irdische vergaß,
zu der stillen Erde sag: Ich rinne.
Zu dem raschen Wasser sprich: Ich bin.

Still friend of many distances, feel yet
how your breathing is augmenting space.
From the beamwork of gloomy belfries let
yourself ring. What devours you will increase

more strongly from this food. Explore and win
knowledge of transformation through and
    through.
What experience was the worst for you?
Is drinking bitter, you must turn to wine.

Be the magic power of this immense
midnight at the crossroads of your senses,
be the purport of their strange meeting.
    Though

earth itself forgot your very name,
say unto the tranquil earth: I flow.
To the fleeting water speak: I am.

NOTES

PART I

1.—In the *Metamorphoses* of Ovid, Book X, Orpheus creates a forest with the music of his lyre. In the present adaptation, the silent animals that, according to lines 9–10, either had been mute before or were suddenly muted by the power of the melody, are now taught to hear for the first time. The tree belongs to the same symbolic wood in which Rilke had long before created another tree, in "Eingang" of *Das Buch der Bilder*, where we find (lines 5-8):

> Then with your eyes that wearily
> scarce lift themselves from the worn-out doorstone
> slowly you raise a shadowy black tree
> and fix it on the sky: slender, alone.

This tree might be called a visual tree and that of Orpheus a tree of sound. The idea is grotesque enough, for an almost Cyclopean ear would have been required. The last sestet, in which the ear is described in terms of a mine entrance, is more accurate and less distressing. The Sonnets as a whole may be said to be a book of Becoming, and the final line of the book reads, "And to the fleeting water speak: I am." Thus, in line 4 "beginnings, signs, and changes" immediately suggest the ideas of metamorphosis, new developments and transformations which eventually justify the conclusion. Rilke has another poem (VIII, p. 99) which ends: "Wir: Hörenden endlich—die ersten Menschen." Next, to this temple of hearing which quite naturally would be dedicated to music and, by extension, to the dance, comes the dedicatée of the poems, the dead girl, Vera.

2.—Angelloz, one of the French translators of the Sonnets, suggests that these first poems make him think of "Le

115

Bois sacré" of Puvis de Chavannes, some of Böcklin's forests peopled with mythological characters, and the young singers of the choir-loft by Luca della Robbia (p. 254). We are all aware of the strong associational power of music to evoke certain memories. The present poem transports the little priestess back to the immediacy of the first poem, and she becomes a handmaid to Orpheus; this allows the poet to include the two subjects he chose, almost arbitrarily it seems, to thrust together. Vera's dancing he had seen only once, and he was not a particularly intimate friend of the mother, but the occasion was too good to be missed. The dancer appears again in Sonnet 15, where she is exhorted to "dance the orange" she has just eaten, and in 25, which deals with her sickness and death and links her again with Orpheus, whose murder is described in 26, the finale of Part I. In Part II she is the subject of another poem, 18, she is dancing the symbol of the "translation of transiency into going," and she has another penultimate poem, 28, where Rilke thanks her for having taught him "the healing meaning of the festival." In the present poem that all-accommodating ear is made to receive a bed! It is this lack of self-criticism which sometimes lays Rilke open, in an almost ridiculous light. "Die gefühlte Wiese" must have been the meadow in which he danced barefooted with Tolstoy's frolicking peasants. When he asks the god to find the motif, he is of course admonishing himself, as Orpheus-Rilke.

3.—This is a restatement of the theory of the origin of poetry to be found on pp. 25–27 of *Malte Laurids Brigge*: " . . . Poetry isn't, as people imagine, merely feelings (these come soon enough); it is experiences." The artist must learn *Selbstvertötung*, the suppression of his ego with its breathless personal emotions, if he is to understand the deepest nature of song which makes of the poet a mouthpiece for the afflatus of the god, "a gust in the god." This explains why so many second-rate poets sing themselves out before middle age; they have felt, but they cannot think. II, 29 reverts to the crossroads theme, which is a symbol for the unification of self with the universal as the passionate human grows toward the transformation into the divine, as Becoming arrives at Being. Faust in the scene before the town gate says:

116

Two souls, alas, live in me: one
wishes to leave its brother;
one with gripping organs clings to earth
with a rough and hearty lust;
the other rises powerfully from the dust
toward the region of the great forefathers.

Baudelaire in "Élévation" praises

Happy the man whose thoughts, like blithe larks flying
in the skies of morning, freely use their powers
—who, hovering over life . . .

and confesses in "Le Gout du Néant" his desire for the
Nothing, which is several steps lower than either of the
alternatives suggested by the two German poets, in his

Avalanche, will you take me in your fall?

"You must find / how to forget your rash song." In
Malte, p. 27, he had written: "But it is not enough to have
memories. One must be able to forget them and have vast
patience until they come again . . . ," and this experience
he must have had repeatedly during the dozen years of
gestation required by the Elegies. Certainly he now felt
that he was able to live up to his line 13: "It is another
breath that sings the truth."

4.—Here he exhorts young girls, and the memory of
Vera in particular, to give themselves to this "breath"
fearlessly. They must not avoid suffering; thus they may
finally become the "great lovers" of the Elegies. They are
the "whole ones" who are doomed to it; but nature—the
mountains, seas, and the trees—is heavy with bearing. Yet
girls should entrust some of their burden to the lighter
elements outside themselves. Here he is in complete accord
with his compatriot, Emil Lucka, whose *Eros* expands
Haeckel's biogenetic law to its fuller psychological implica-
tions, as far as men are concerned, but he insists that
women have always been closer to life and that their love
has always been independent of sexuality. The Elegies
contain several fuller statements of similar theses, and a
drop of their essence has been used for the present son-

117

net. With the figure of the bow and arrow compare the First Elegy, lines 52–53,

> As the arrow stands the bowstring, tensed to be *more* than itself
> in the leap of its flight.

5.—Orpheus, torn and parceled into all nature (Sonnet 26), is thus capable of all sorts of metamorphosis. The rose was Rilke's favorite flower, and it is as this symbol that he expects the eternity of the god, or of song, to be manifested. Without arrogance he naturally speaks somewhat to himself, even when he speaks directly of the god as poet. Both must die and vanish so that the remaining word may assume its due importance. Everything that sings is Orpheus, and all the poets, of course, are in the chorus. Whether the disobedience implied in the last line refers to the descent of Orpheus to Hades, or his subsequent failure in releasing Eurydice, or whether it means that a poet may seem to break laws and traditions—for instance, in his technique and ideology—is difficult to say. He may well be in accord with some higher and unwritten law. In *Neue Gedichte*, "Die Rosenschale," "Das Roseninnere," and "Persisches Heliotrop" give other interpretations of Rilke's use of the rose as symbol. The Sonnets II, 5, 6, 7, 14, and 21 carry on this floral device until the whole book looks like a lyre surrounded by a wreath of blossoms. Leishman felicitously calls this poem "A Poet's Epitaph."

6.—According to the legend, on his journey into Hades Orpheus carried a bough of willow as a talisman. If the modern poet wishes to avail himself of symbols in the second realm (a constant theme in the Elegies), they must be made real and loved in the realm of the living, somewhat as the Lares and Penates were assumed to be at home in the simple daily objects about the house. The pitcher occurs again in II, 15 and 18. The other relics are similar to those in "Hetärengräber" in N.G. The bread and milk on the table were used previously by Valéry in "Palme" of the *Poésies*. Fumitory and rue are typical graveyard flora and will remind readers of various lines from Shakespeare. According to Hartmann Goertz, p. 101, Rilke is creating

118

in these poems "the mythos of his own life," even though some of the Sonnets are sung *for* and some *by* Orpheus.

7.—Here we find the theme of the Seventh Elegy and a statement of the beginning of the Tenth:

> May I some day at the exit of grim understanding
> sing out jubilation and lauds to affirmative angels!

And the "Praise the world to the angel" of the Seventh. To praise is the duty to which the poet comes ordained. He must be able to transmute everything in his alembic. He must be the strong winepress, the abundant vineyard; he must be unperturbed by death or fate and must believe that poetry is stronger than death and that his praise, as symbolized by the fruit he reaches *past* the door of death itself, is of more enduring stuff than his own mortality. Behind this sonnet works the constant assurance of the Elegies: this faculty of understanding is not developed until after the full acceptance of pain and lamentation. How much more humane and lovable is such a god, or poet, than that other vintner who is "pressing out the vintage where the grapes of wrath are stored"! But then, Rilke is a poet and not a propagandist.

8.—In his re-creation of an Orphic world Rilke needed a little pantheon: the sisterhood of the emotions, feelings, sentiments (*Gemüt*), and later in the Tenth Elegy we find a whole country dominated by the Laments. Precipitation is here used in its exact sense and implies the final clarity produced in a solution in which the dregs have settled. If *frühen* can be used as a verb, Muret-Sanders forgot to list it in their dictionary. It is here used figuratively for "it dawns." The "rocky base on which the gates and altars stand" may be interpreted as being the essential human nature that in its more noble endeavors has erected cities and temples. The other sisters have learned their duty: to praise. But the younger, the apprentice, is still employed (almost as a menial) in counting the evils. Her protest is fine when she takes the voices of men as she hears them—in sorrow and lamentation, in other words, in their best threnodies and dirges, their lyrics of sorrow—and creates a new constellation in which art and beauty

119

supersede the hysteria of violent grief and undisciplined wailings. In this very principle of giving an order to human experience, she is initiated completely into the circle of the god.

9.—Here a mortal neophyte to the guild of the Praisers is presented. He is the poet who "has eaten his bread in tears," as Goethe insists all must do who would know the heavenly powers. The third stanza is a Platonic figure: the reflection in this world of the eternal image in that of the Ideas. This type of short-line sonnet was probably suggested by those of Baudelaire, Mallarmé, and Valéry. Of course, the journey of Orpheus to Hades stimulated the octave, but it seems preferable to make the chastening and elevating effects of sorrow more universal and humanly achievable.

10.—The magnificent fountains of Rome—whose prototypes were supplied by the aqueducts from the Apennines (see II, 15)—always fascinated Rilke. The sarcophagi themselves had already had a poem in N.G., "Römische Sarkophage," where we read:

Then from the ancient aqueducts—oh, then
eternal water would be turned into them—:
which glitters there and goes and gleams again.

Those of the second stanza are from the famous Road of Tombs among the Roman ruins at Les Alyscamps, near Arles, where many of the open coffins have collected enough dust to offer a few weeds their hospitality. I could discover no dead-nettle, but some of them were half full of sycamore leaves. Two predecessors have stuffed them otherwise: one with "honeyed thighs," whatever that may mean; the second with "bee-balm," a charming menthaceous plant, which, however, seems to have no relation to the dead-nettles of the original. But the point of the sonnet is that coffins employed in any other fashion than for inhumation have been "delivered from doubt . . . aware what silence means." Death has achieved a beauty which passes from the living water and the silent flowers and butterflies into the face of man. The "lingering hour" of line 13 is like that one found in "Das Kind" in N.G., from which comes the following:

Without intending it, they watch his play
a long while, and sometimes a living round
face turns from the profile and straightway
is clear and full: an hour, about to sound
completion with uplifted blow.

Angelloz (p. 261) suggests that the sarcophagi have learned
the teachings of death and therefore help to mold the face
of man on which lingers the hour "of hesitation" to know
and accept the second realm.

11.—In the Tenth Elegy the poet also, apparently with
benefit of Arabian astronomy, created a sidereal galaxy for
his purpose: The Rider, The Staff, Garland of Fruit,
Cradle, Reed, The Burning Book, Doll, and Window. Here
he singles out "Der Reiter" as a symbol for man's duality.
He refers to the two stars at the crook of the handle of the
Dipper: Alcor, a fourth-magnitude star—the name was cor-
rupted from the Arabian for "courser,"—is visible to sharp
eyes only and was once used as a test for applicants into
the army. If an Arab didn't want to risk death for Maho-
met's sake and for the raptures of the heaven of houris, he
simply couldn't see Alcor at all! Mizar is a greenish-white
second-magnitude star and would seem more naturally to
be the horse of the couple, although the name originally
meant the "loincloth" which was regarded as draping the
modest Bear. In Latin the combination was known as "The
Little Starry Horseman" (*Eques stellula*), and in English
as "Jack on the Middle Horse." Rilke probably had it from
one of these rather than from the Arabic or the German
name, which is "Hans Thumbkin" and wouldn't have done
at all. He uses the symbol somewhat as Plato employs the
two horses that pull the chariot of the soul. It is not
clear in the poem whether Rilke does not expect some sort
of centaur-like creature to develop, but he had made an-
other symbol to express his dual worlds.

12.—This is too mixed up to afford much poetic satisfac-
tion. The clock, the radio stations, and the peasant in the
field make an unsatisfactory hash. True, there is our own
personal time, daylight-saving time, and time in the Berg-
sonian sense. The antennae do vibrate with pure tension
and convey some sort of music, and the farmer benefits
from nature without understanding its workings. If Rilke

121

is attempting a compromise, to establish contact with the absolutes, he has not got very far on the way.

13.—Now come three poems dealing with fruit. The theme of the first is indebted to Valéry's "Le Cimetière marin," from which the fifth stanza reads:

> As the fruit by its very dissolution
> is transformed to delight and gratification
> within the mouth and loses its first form,
> here I breathe in the phantom of my future . . .

In the Fourth Elegy, lines 78–81:

> . . . Who makes the child's death
> out of the gray bread that gets hard—or leaves it there
> in the round mouth like the core of a pretty apple? . . .

Here we have an attempt to deal honestly with the intangibility of an ordinary pleasant taste. It is an example of the theme of metamorphosis which belongs to the legend.

14.—Here again is a debt, this time a greater one, to Valéry's poem, especially from stanzas 13–21, too long for quotation. A few comparisons must suffice. In the present sonnet, lines 7–8,

> This long time they have larded through and through
> the clay, with the frank marrow of their bones . . . ,

almost duplicate Valéry's

> They have coalesced into a heavy absence,
> and the red clay has drunk the white clay's substance,
> the knack of living has passed into the flowers!

Similarly

> Out of the dark a pied display appears

pleasantly resembles

> . . . but from their marble-laden night a levy
> of dim folk from the trees' roots comes.

Here the dead are transmuted into the forces of earth and give back tithes of fruit to the living. Maybe they are slaves, maybe they are arrogant masters who merely toss crumbs from their abundance.

15.—This study of the nutritional and aesthetic value of orange juice is too precious to have much poetic merit. Briefly, the girls eat some orange; now they must dance it. "Exquisitely it has become you" suggests further digestive processes that make the poem silly. Yet I have read a criticism which alleges that the poet is here "using the five-fingered hand of his senses." (This is a phrase from his dull essay, "Ur-Geräusch," in which he advances the theory that a phonograph needle might be used to play the cranial sutures!) When Rilke is bad, he is exceedingly bad. It is not clear whether the dance occurs in Italy or in the chilly north. I prefer the latter idea, because then there is some reason for the projection of the warmer land. Valéry's essay, "L'Ame et la danse," maintains that the dancer is "the pure act of the metamorphoses."

16.—There is a better dog poem in N.G., "Der Hund." Line 5 reminds me of William James's query: Who can tell what pleasure a dog experiences as he runs along hedges, sniffing at old bones and fenceposts? The idea of the poem is that the dog has powers not allowed to man and therefore is necessary to complete man's faculties, while the dog needs man for his affection. Rilke, however, refused to have a dog in the lonely tower of Duino because, he said, "I would find myself giving the animal little pieces of my heart, then bigger ones." (Like dog biscuits!) There wouldn't be anything left for the poetry, he alleged. The Biblical reference is used for an analogy. Rilke says: You are the true heir of Isaac (Orpheus). I shall take you to my master, lay his hand on your fell, and he will recognize you (Esau). M. D. Herter Norton's note on this piece is particularly informative, and Professor J. B. Leishman, with his customary scholarly astuteness, presents a whole dog-show in his annotation.

17.—Behind the poet is the racial heritage, the family tree—not to be confused with that in the first sonnet. Each branch is a man destined to perform deeds of war, the chase, the forum, or a woman like a musical instrument re-

123

sembling a mandolin. This last is very bad, for a woman so shaped nowadays would be regarded by any male with the gravest apprehension. The poet is, of course, the top twig. Maybe this ladder-tree was suggested by Jacob's dream; the Bible may have stimulated these two so different poems at the same time.

18.—This is the first of several poems dealing with the machine age. See 22, 23, and 24. But in a book dedicated to a dead danseuse and evoking the god of music they seem entirely extraneous, riveted on, as it were, like little metal warts. Ruskin and Morris would have agreed with this indictment of the machine. Incidentally, Rilke was consistent, for he refused to have the tower of Muzot modernized.

19.—Even in this whirring world which progresses by leaps and bounds we must not lose sight of our debt to the cultural poet. Only song can consecrate the works of man and attend them with praise. Bertallot in his essay, "Der Sinn des Orpheus-Symbols," writes: "An important question is here raised: Can beauty maintain its stand before the terror of the Eternal? . . . Art as a savior of the world from the curse of destruction in the presence of the Infinite—that is the meaning of the Orpheus-symbol." This is typical Germanic *Schwärmerei*, this business of the "Eternal" and the "Infinite," but against the evils of the present age we may at least hope, however vainly, that art will console us on the way out.

20.—This is wholly delightful and restores my faith in the poet. It is perhaps the best lyric about nature in the book, and it gives the whole arduous business of sniffing after another man's trail up Parnassus an almost picnic mood. He saw this horse at the time of his Russian interlude (when he ran barefooted in the morning dew for a few days, hobnobbed and ate with the peasants and piously kissed them, his little brothers in God, et cetera). But the poem is only slight compensation for his servile but brash attitude in pursuing Tolstoy, nor does it make up for his too elaborate pretenses in *Das Stundenbuch*, one of his most artificial lapses. In *Briefe aus Muzot* (pp. 102–103) he wrote: "And only fancy, one thing more . . . I wrote, created the horse . . . the happy, carefree white horse,

124

hobbled by the fetlock, that once came galloping to us, just before evening, in a meadow by the Volga." And to Clara Rilke, in 1923: "Isn't that white horse charming? After all, nothing is lost!" The poem is an interesting contrast to the unicorn, II, 4, and I must note that these two and II, 15 are the only poems in the book cast in hard masculine monosyllabic rhymes. Mason (pp. 192–193) writes: "Perhaps the most moving poem of Rilke, in which he celebrates his favorite condition of *In-sich-Seines*, no longer without limitations and lost beyond the grave among formidable angels, but wholly drawn into the bounds of our present world."

21.—In one of the few personal notes published with the sonnets he writes: "The little spring poem is to me . . . an interpretation of some wonderful dance music I heard sung by children in the convent . . . at Ronda, in southern Spain." It is naïve and childlike, but, aside from the last two lines, hardly worth printing. A score of better spring songs by German Romantics are readily recalled. Nature as a teacher sounds like diluted Wordsworth. But the little primer printed in hieroglyphics of roots and stems which is to be read as music is priceless. Cf. II, 25 for a companion poem.

22, 23, 24.—These make a series devoted to warnings that we, especially the younger people, should avoid being caught in the vertiginous swirl of the machine. The swift and transient is not the abiding; "Alles vergängliche / ist nur ein Gleichniss" is a better poem on a somewhat similar theme and suggested the verse rhythm. The sound of the 12 long *i*'s of the original I have vaguely imitated in my first stanza. The flyer should consider the goal rather than the flight; here the emphasis is again on Becoming as the apprenticeship to Being, an Orphic doctrine. The last and best of the series asks what man's future will be since he has deserted the gods for the machine. In hurried modern life, too busy for the leisurely feasts and baths of the ancients, man has lost contact not only with his fellows, but with the gods themselves. (We have almost forgotten the mythopoeic era when nymphs, angels, and even the gods walked the earth, took part in our battles, sometimes intermarried among us.) As for roads, compare the autostrada

125

between Milan and Turin with the charm of the Grande Corniche along the Côte d'Azur. Fire as symbol of man's attempt to reach the gods is now merely practical. Like swimmers far from shore, we are in danger.

25.—Finally (and it is high time) he addresses a poem to Vera. She had died of some glandular disease, with complications and hemorrhages; perhaps there had been paralysis. The poet triumphs over this unusual material and creates a very strange sort of poetry. No longer able to dance, she is, as it were, "cast in bronze" in the swift swirl of that tree of motion accomplished by the dancer in II, 18 or in "Spanische Tänzerin" (cf. Introduction). The dark music of the gods, still powerful enough to take us from life, has frozen her to a sculptural memory. The purposely short final line is one of his best: that eternally open gate of death at which there is slight need to knock (the terrible pounding of the blood) in order to gain admittance. Notice that the subject of the sestet is not the girl, but the blood. The poet has created a disquieting supernatural mood in making this disembodied blood, dark, surging, glittering, finally visible, almost like the girl herself before the gate.

26.—Having given him the dead dancer as high priestess, the poet can now round off the first part with the death of his hero. Again Ovid affords the factual stimulus. Like any savior, Orpheus must die before his divinity can become valid for the doubting Thomases. Remember the fate of Osiris, Adonis, hundreds of Indian fertility gods, and Jesus. Orpheus in the first poem created temples in the hearing; now, after his death, he is parceled throughout nature, thus finally giving it a voice. A disciple of Apollonian art: "Song . . . is not passion," Orpheus is naturally hated by the Dionysian Maenads with their hysterical orgiastic shrieking. (They kill him as easily as bop has killed Bach in modern America.) All anarchistic principles try to overthrow the ordered music of the classical tradition. But the latter has yet triumphed because Orpheus' song is still to be heard through all nature. Mason (p. 189) says that Rilke once thought of including the Head and Lyre as one of the constellations in the Tenth Elegy. And I believe it was Odilon Redon who did some very dismal pictures of the floating head. But for-

126

tunately, Orpheus survives for our times, symbolized by no such agonizing details, tortures, mayhem, *et al.*, but as a simple lyre.

PART II

1.—If Orpheus, like Osiris, underwent dismemberment in order to effect a more essential unification of self with nature, the poet is here concerned with the relation between his own breath and space. Each partakes of the other: he creates by occupation vacuums and by respiration the winds, and the air gives form to his words, as the rind shows the shape of a fruit. This ocean of air is reminiscent of the song of the Earth-spirit in *Faust*:

Ein ewiges Meer,
Ein wechselnd Weben.

And Valéry in "Cimetière marin" has "la mer toujours recommencée." Angelloz (p. 277) points out the analogy of the tree of hearing in I, 1, with the tree in the last tercet for which the air makes the bark and foliage of the words. There is naturally a constant temptation on Rilke's part to identify himself with the god of song, so it is here probably Rilke-Orpheus who is singing.

2.—Even as the god lost his life, our experience is also full of losses. Here are three examples. The painter's "genuine" stroke is interfered with by a hasty leaf which touches the brush; thus the masterpiece fails to be created. The girls smile in the mirrors, that "one blessed smile," their real faces, but these are quickly dimmed and a mere reflection of girl remains. In the first tercet he considers all the visions one has seen in the black frame of the fireplace: visions quickly lost as the coals sink and blacken. The sonnet closes: despite these eternal losses, the poet must praise, nevertheless, and thus enter into deeper understanding. One must lose in order to gain. This insistence on the necessity of praise despite suffering is a major Rilkean theme, both in the Sonnets and in the Elegies. It is his form of whistling in the dark. Praise the unity behind diversity, the noumenon behind the phenomena.

3.—In the Greek Anthology there is a charming poem on a mirror, but my copy is six thousand miles away.

Though there's nothing inside and it's empty as air,
It is plain to be seen that there's everything there.

The mirror, like a sieve, is full of holes, the "interstices of time" during which nothing passes to be reflected. It wastes its time on the empty hall; it is easily pierced by the sharp lights of the chandelier, as by the horns of an eight-year-old stag. Angelloz suggests that line 9 refers to the trick which painters use when they look at their pictures in a mirror, to catch faults. Those that "have entered" into the mirror may perhaps be the imagined faces of those who are dead if one gazes in mirrors they have once used. Narcissus, that eternally self-hypnotized gazer, complicates matters. Valéry has done two poems and a late cantata on the subject. Rilke gave him a poem in *Späte Gedichte*, and his French poems have a few lines:

    . . . invente le thème
    du Narcisse exaucé.

The girl with unkissed cheeks in the last section is finally reached by Narcissus, but what the poet intended is not clear to me. There is a contrast between the partition of Orpheus and the egoistic concentration of the self-lover. Rilke bewailed several times that he feared he was a mirror rather than a person.

4.—If the girl in the last poem and the virgin here link the two, so much the better. Maybe the fictitious animal is presented as contrast to the very real little horse in I, 20. Anyhow, it is one of Rilke's pet subjects. "Das Einhorn" in N.G. has no relation to this one, but another equally hypothetical origin for the creature is given in "Mariä Verkündigung" of the *Marienleben*, from which I translate:

    Oh, if we knew how pure she was! A hind
    once on a time lying in a wood,
    beheld her and, bemused by gazing, could—
    all without any coupling with her kind—
    conceive the unicorn, pure animal,
    the beast of light.

128

Parthogenetic though this origin may be, it is more satisfactory than the merely imaginary one of the present poem. Whatever the antecedents of the animal may or may not have been, he has long since achieved a definite reality in the famous tapestries of the Musée de Cluny, "La Dame à la licorne," six glowing, colored masterpieces of the Middle Ages. In *Malte*, Rilke wrote of them, and I shall quote from *The Journal of My Other Self*, the translation by John Linton, because I have not the original by me (p. 122): "But here is yet another festival; no one is invited to it. Expectation plays no part in it. Everything is here. Everything forever. The lion looks around almost threateningly: no one may come. We have never seen her weary before; is she weary? Or is she merely resting because she holds something heavy? A monstrance, one might say. But she curves her other arm towards the unicorn, and the flattered animal bridles and rears and leans against her lap. It is a mirror that she holds. See! She is showing the unicorn its likeness." The dominant colors of these tapestries are old rose for the background and cobalt blue for a sort of island on which the lady, the unicorn, and a lion appear. Both background and island are planted to trees and flowers and overrun by hundreds of charming and amusing animals and birds. The following is my own comment on the particular tapestry referred to:

There is no peace here. The blue isle grows small,
with two dwarfed trees, as if to force the eye
to focus on the mirror where he poses:

his docile hoofs in the young lap, his tall
horn rampant proudly, as he blandly gazes
at the bright image of eternal I . . .

and in her weary hand
she holds the mirror; with a half caress
the other lies upon his argent neck.

Her face is sad because she understands
the expected gestures—and her gentleness
is fleshed upon the pliant bones of tact.
Cafés and Cathedrals

Perhaps the one connection between the first four poems of this section is the fact that in all of them Rilke is insisting on the necessity of attempting to be. By breathing and occupying space we become part of the air. In 2 by our very losses we become part of the All. In 3 the mirror gets its reality when Narcissus penetrates it and stays there; it is no longer a mere reflector of things. The unicorn is thought into reality and finally achieves it by entering into both the mirror and the real girl. It is not necessary to go into all the implicit symbolism suggested here. Odell Shepard's *The Lore of the Unicorn* is the best study I know on the fabulous animal, and the curious reader should not overlook it. A further connection between the poem and the series is the idea that the god and the young dancer have entered reality by death, as the unicorn has come into space and reality.

5.—In a very maudlin letter to his cousin, the poet says that he is like an anemone which has opened so far that it could not close at night! As far as I am concerned, that leaves him wide open in two ways. But the pathetic fallacy in this sonnet is not so bad as the sentimentality personally expressed in the letter. Man must learn, even as the flower's example teaches, to be receptive to external influences. This theme is taken up fully in the Eighth Elegy. The idea of reincarnation in line 13 is unusual in the poet's work. This sonnet is full of magnificent polysyllabic musical words, and is one of the best, as far as sheer poetry goes, in the book. And a 22-letter word is rarely met with, even in German. Incidentally, when a flower is too tired to fold up at night, it has already done so for good, as any botanist would agree.

6.—In *N.G.*, "Persisches Heliotrop," we find:

Es könnte sein, daß dir der Rose Lob
zu laut erscheint . . .

"It could be that you think the rose has been overpraised." Yet here he lauds it again. In most poems the simple five-petaled rose is used, but here the modern, blushing, cabbage-like monstrosity is precisely indicated. J. A. Symonds has a delightful essay on the subject, "The Pathos of the Rose."

Surely no other flower has quite the rich associational power to project man's mind back in time. In *Poèmes français* there is a poem in "Vergers" which reads:

> On arrange et on compose
> les mots de tant de façons,
> mais comment arriverait-t-on
> à egaler une rose?
>
> Si on supporte l'étrange
> prétention de ce jeu,
> c'est que parfois un ange
> le dérange un peu.

And that means something like this:

> One arranges and one composes
> the words and fashions his theme,
> but how will he ever scheme
> to equal the real roses?
>
> If one can sustain this play
> with its strange pretentions, it
> is because some angel may
> have mussed it up a bit.

By one of the apparently malevolent ironies that crop up so often, this man who so loved roses scratched his hand while tending the flowers in his garden at Muzot, and the ensuing infection led to the discovery, by a hitherto strangely ignorant doctor, that he was already suffering from leukemia, of which he died shortly thereafter, in 1926, aged 51. Let us not neglect the eloquent documentation of Angelloz on this sonnet (p. 281): "The anemone is a flower which welcomes infinity, but the rose is a queen who closes herself on her own richness. . . . She is no longer for us, as for antiquity, the simple eglantine. . . . Her body is only a luminous void comparable to the invisible axis around which the dancer coils her metamorphoses. . . . Rilke said one day that he wished someone would name a variety of rose after him."

131

7.—The sweet sisterhood of young girls and flowers, worn to the thinness of a cliché by hundreds of poets, is here rejuvenated. This is the last of a series of flower poems that balances the one on fruits in Part I. The young girls join the piece to the series on the dead dancer. Picked flowers are already dead, but the fresh water—and the delicate fingers—revive them for a while. They even gain an increased loveliness, he alleges, from the contact with the living girls. The forcing of the flowers to be accomplices to the sin of being picked is a pathetic fallacy hard to take. One is reminded of the speaking flowers of Goethe ("Heidenröslein"), and Tennyson ("Come into the garden, Maud . . ."), and Hugo's dialogue between the rose and the grave. The only vocal flower I ever heard was a snapdragon that said "Pop!" when it opened. But the theme, the ephemerality of all loveliness, floral as well as human, relates it to the death of her of the musical name, Wera Ouckama Knoop.

8.—The death of this cousin has been remembered elsewhere, in *Malte*, where he is the prototype of Erik Brahe, and in the Fourth Elegy, "der Knabe nicht mehr mit dem braunen Schielaug." Here is a fine understanding of the love of privacy among children. They merely shut a silent door on one, and there he stands—outside a transparent plastic wall, far away as Arcturus. Line 4 refers to the altarpieces, such as that of the Van Eycks in Ghent, in which the Lamb of God has a scroll in his mouth, with a pious motto. Like the children, he communicates without having to speak. Rilke's childhood had been badly upset by a doting but flighty mother, and the schools he had attended in Prague and at St. Pölten. In this play near swarming streets and foreboding alien houses, only the ball had reality. As a symbol of transiency, of eternal rising and falling, it relates to the short life of the boy to whom it is dedicated, and therefore to the girl Wera. The final line is particularly clumsy, even for German, because it seems as if the boy had been killed by a falling ball. This is unforgivably bad writing: one of the results of doing a book after a few weeks of "dictation," without sufficient revision. He has another poem about balls in *Späte Gedichte*, "Solang du selbst-geworfenes fängst . . . ," cf. Günther, pp. 51, 194, 275.

9.—Abruptly we meet a change of subject matter which is carried on in 11. All the apparent clemency in the treatment of criminals, says Rilke, has merely been forced on the judges whose consciences hurt them. The real god of mercy would have come as mightily as the great winds at sea, and have overcome the world as gently as one is charmed by the silent play of a child who is not aware of being watched. Rilke considered Christ as "an obstacle on the road toward God." Also he insisted that the angels of the Elegies were like those of Islam and not at all like the Christian type. Line 6 is fine, nor is this a trick of childhood only—haven't we all given away ties from last Christmas? I have visited many museums that bristled with instruments of torture: racks, Spanish boots, thumbscrews, sharp-spined horses on which the culprit sat with weights on his feet, water cures, Iron Maidens, guillotines, gibbets, beheading-swords and axes, et cetera. Most of them were applied to one victim at a time. Nowadays we can do the thing wholesale.

10.—This is the same theme as that in I, 18, 22–24, and none of them have anything to do with his subject. It neither requires nor deserves annotation. Only the last tercet saves it. This music springing from the stones made vocal by Orpheus can erect a grander mansion in space than can any machine fabricated by man. The Seventh Elegy uses similar material, but what has the present poem to do with the death of Wera? It is, of course, not bad as a contrast of the mechanistic and the idealistic points of view.

11.—This is a strange poem, justifying the wholesale slaughter of birds, a touch of sadism almost; but Rilke's pseudo-metaphysical attitude toward death must be remembered. And if death is the culmination of man's life, the Good Thing, it must be grand for birdies too. Death may very well be "the other side of life," and a wise acceptance of it is finally learned by everyone; but I wonder if he ever held a dying bird in his hand, watched the eyes glaze with terror and pain and the claws clench and stiffen in that final clutch at nothing. Where is all his sentimentality for flowers? The caverns of Karst are near Duino, Trieste, where the elegies had been begun twelve years prior to this time. Markets in Italy often feature a windowful of dead small birds, on platters, garnished with parsley: larks, robins, thrushes, not merely game birds. Axel Munthe established a bird sanctuary at Anacapri, one of the few places in the Mediterranean where a migrating bird can go to sleep with the assurance that he will not be speedily en-balmed in a pastry coffin. Vernon Lee in *Ariadne in Mantua* has two essays on the maltreatment of birds in Italy. The poem concludes rather lamely that whatever is is right. Mason (p. 185) says that the Sonnets, more than any other of Rilke's works, were occasioned by a kind of mystic-unconditional guilt feeling—but on a very unusual pantheistic level. In justifying the slaughter the poet is relieving one of his complexes. In *Rilke et Benvenuta* (Denoël, Paris, 1947), p. 68, the heroine reports: "I had supposed that Rilke, like myself, would passionately op-pose hunting. But, friendly as he is to animals, he under-stands it and he explained that it demonstrates the power of atavism in man; that even the cruelty and desire to kill are deeply rooted in human nature. . . . The original motive of hunger has been exchanged for a feeling of power."

12.—Six-foot lines in German, even with Goethe, are usually bad, and here some of the lines are irregular. The theme of transformation is also a major idea in the Elegies. Man must not only accept change, but must purpose, wel-come, and praise it. Without it, the spirit grows stiff and numb. The hammer of time or fate is always raised for the ultimate blow. One must pour himself out like spring. He must live with "hand ever at his lips, bidding adieu." Daphne is a symbol of life after transformation—you re-member her tree-change was occasioned by her fear of Apollo. Angelloz points out Goethe's

> Und so lang' du das nicht hast,
> Dieses: Stirb und werde!
> Bist du nur ein trüber Gast
> Auf der dunklen Erde.
> > *West-östlicher Divan*, "Selige Sehnsucht"

All this is somewhat of a piece with the Oriental ideas of transmigration of souls. The present sonnet invokes fire, water, and air as media of effecting the change. The last tercet is reminiscent of II, 1. Stanza 2 implies that lack of

134

change creates numbness, crystallization into a hard substance, but the hammer of destruction is still harder. Therefore be changed by fire, become water or air. Daphne by her metamorphosis becomes a sort of priestess to Orpheus, who has completely imbued nature with himself.

13.—The willingness to accept change, in the foregoing poem, now culminates in advice to meet death open-armed. Man must wish to advance from the eternal winteriness of life into eternal life—of exactly what sort the poet does not say. This series was written during February. The four repetitions of "winter" are worse than "when first my eye I eyed." Line 8 is the best line he ever wrote, both as music and idea: death in the full verve of life. Eurydice, as the dead wife of Orpheus, seems to imply that the deaths of those dear to us increase our capacity to feel suffering, hence, to sing as poets in praise of sorrow. When man wills to add himself to the total of dead, he destroys the smug total and thus creates change (transformation?) in death itself. Or such the meaning seems to me.

14.—Rilke's philosophy about "Things" has very little in common with the *Ding-an-sich*. Like everyone else, he apparently was attached to certain objects which meant something as symbols. But his notion that the inanimate objects of nature are childishly happy and that man should emulate them is a bit too precious for my gorge. The Seventh Elegy is much in the same spirit. There is something almost Wordsworthian here in this acceptance of Things and nature and the idea that we should be like the flowers. This all smacks of escapism. Rilke's continual flight from reality and obligations—and his life is a diary of that—led him astray, and he had no right to enspell the reader with the seductive music of his verse and then inoculate him with his often unmanly ideas. Perhaps that is part of his virtue: we rebel against his softness and steel the muscles of our souls. Though "shades of the prison house begin to close about the growing boy," he needn't necessarily want to become a daffodil.

15.—One of the best in the book, a fine example of structural use of a symbol to unify a series of poems. We have seen Orpheus teaching nature to hear, I, 1, and in I, 26 man becomes finally a mouth, a singer himself. And nature, too, can now sing to herself, as the fountain's basin becomes an ear. The piece is interesting because the marmoreal fountains might have been purely *parnassien* material, but Rilke has made them into the liquid music of Symbolism, as Mallarmé taught his disciples how to do —and Rilke was profoundly influenced by the little master of the Rue de Rome. Here is light, sound, motion—the thing lives and vibrates. There is even some humor where the eternal chatterer is interrupted by the interposed pitcher. Europe still has many of these public fountains where women fill their pitchers—as well as galvanized iron pails. Those "marching aqueducts," alas, are really ruins, because more practical syphon systems have been installed. Even that sublime aqueduct of Claudius nowadays

> . . . since time put it by, this caravan
> of sculptured elephants without a load,
> save ghostly water in its dusty veins,
> sleeps toward oblivion.

Rome has still several hundred fountains which are never turned off. The simpler ones are more impressive than the large bowls in the great squares. Who does not love the pine-cone fountain, or the one with four papal tiaras where the donkeys and dogs can drink, or that shell where the stone bees are drinking, or the most delicate one where the young boys are giving water to their tortoises?

16.—Life, with its curiosity and struggle, leads directly to pain; only the god is serene. Man is a cutting sharpness, trying to get ahead in the world. The god, having been disparted through nature, has become something universal. Motionlessly—wise passiveness, because he does not need to use his forces, since he conquers by his nonresistance—he accepts the libations of the living. They, on the contrary, get nothing of the boon of death, only its sound. Only the dead really partake of the divine melody. In the last lines the simple animal, glad to accept its destiny, asks for its bell. (I believe I have seen dogs that actually wanted to have their collars on before taking a walk.) This is quite in the spirit of the Eighth Elegy. But E. M. Butler (p. 357) calls this sonnet "a lapse into pure inanity." Oh, well—*de gustibus* . . . Man may well make sacrifices to the god; the god accepts them but does not allow the offerant full knowledge of himself until after death. The lamb, naturally a meek beast, follows willingly what it has been taught. It is without care, happy to be guided, unaware of death (Eighth Elegy), a perfectly adjusted creature. Only man, the eternal recalcitrant, must really suffer.

17.—After the realistic parks of N.G., Rilke becomes the artist who creates the strange landscapes of the Tenth Elegy and the enchanted gardens of this sonnet and 21. Immortal gardens, almost like those of the Hesperides, they await the dead with a serenity surpassing mortal understanding. Man might as well be cheerful about it! The poem is one of consolation to the mother of Wera. Grief has ripened into sorrow in the symbol of a marvelous fruit. Most people gradually learn this lesson: after the violence of the first shock, the long numbness of healing, and finally, the purified and always glorified memory which, though it evokes a long sigh, always leaves an inexpressible sadness and sweetness . . . as when one thinks of a dead mother, lost long ago. But these darling Fra Angelico angels, roosting in fruit trees, like so many birds, are far from those "terrible" angels of the Elegies.

18.—Since Kaufmann (pp. 51 ff.) has done such a thorough job with this sonnet, I shall base the following on his annotation. Apparently it meant much more to him than to me. He discovers traces of Mallarmé's *Divagations* and Valery's "L'Ame et la danse," and even similarities with Keats's "Grecian Urn." In I, 15, we found the girl dancing the orange, projecting from herself the vista of the warmer climate that had grown the fruit. The word "transiency" plunges us into the flux of life which always swirls us off without our being able to arrest it. Then comes the dancer who translates this transiency into an immediate action of the dance, fixes it, one might say, as a small climax, a little waypoint in time. (We have seen movement suddenly stop, swirl, and poise motionlessly. We are richer by an image, an image which assures us of some duration even of the instant, an erected and beautiful tree, a pitcher twirled on the potter's wheel: two images that give us some feeling of duration.) This is related to the tree erected by Orpheus in the first sonnet. A whole year of practice has been melted into this figure; it has been a difficult year, full of vast effort and strain, a "hard-swung year," someone has called it. And the bees, the makers of nature's sweetest gift, hang in clusters from this beautifully modeled—and purely instantaneous—tree. And all the warmth of the young girl has gone into its creation. Rilke had translated Valéry's "L'Ame et la danse," in which the dancer Athikté finishes her dance and sinks down, half dead, half alive. Socrates asks whence she has come. She replies, "Sanctuary, O my refuge! O whirlwind!—I was *in* you, O motion, and outside of everything else." (Now I can get back on my own again.) The striped pitcher is suggested by the whirling line of the girl's dark brows and eyes: as if a brush had been held against a clay pot spun on the wheel. Kaufmann wants to read these "ripened stripes" as the rings of a developing tree, but this seems wrong to me. Rilke has passed by the tree and has decorated it, almost like a Christmas tree, with pitcher and vase. These take the stripes of color, like Greek pots. Compare this with a similar finale of a dance in the Introduction: "Spanische Tänzerin" (p. xii), and the bronze figure created in I, 25.

19.—This seems pretty far-fetched to me, as out of place as a Queen Mary hat in a fashion show. In fact, it is stupid to have written it for this series of poems, although it could well have stood on its own in another book. It is a sociological poem about wealth and poverty, and only the dragging in of Orpheus by the hair, at the end, justifies in a feeble fashion its inclusion here. In brief, it reads to me like: The poor ye have always with you. *Alors!* No! Rilke is often as careless as a sleeping child who forgets himself. But beggars appear in *Malte* and in poems like that about the blind man on the Pont des Arts. Paris is a Mecca for eleemosynaries. The several carved hands of Rodin no doubt taught the poet this impressive use of the isolated single image to create a symbol of all mendicity.

20.—Arnold's stanzas on isolation are much better: "Yea, on the sea of life, enisled, / We mortal millions live alone." But it's pleasing, that bit about the fleeing girl who is actually chasing the man, in her own fashion. However, those faces of fish, probably boiled fish, at that; served complete, maybe breaded with crumbs, a slice of lemon, or bordelaise sauce—all this fatuity dragged into a poem about stars, being, and love! And the final whimsy of

138

ichthyological dialogues carried on with moist labials amounting to silvery bubbles of zero is pure bathos. Anyhow, fish do talk; I have heard them while diving for abalone.

21.—After a hail of praise for the fabulous, inaccessible gardens of Asia, he turns—as in the Sixth Elegy—to the ripe fig tree with which his heart is perfectly at home. Lines 9–10 are litotic, of course: in other words, actually be brave enough to decide *to be*. That is a silken thread in the whole woven carpet which is a complete existence in and after life. Stefan George (Vol. 5) presents a similar idea in "Der Teppich." Here we see the vision of the whole carpet. I quote from stanza 2, without punctuation, as in the original:

> With rich embroidery in naked lines
> the parts confuse each other in their strife
> an interlacing riddle none divines
> until one evening the work comes to life . . .

and the poem concludes: the vision of the whole is not intended for everyone,

> Is never for the many never through speech
> and to the rare folk rarely and in vision.

I feel sure that Rilke had read this. He concludes that even a whole earthly life of grief is but a small thing to some vaster eye.

22.—In spite of the pain of life mentioned in the preceding poem, existence is still rich in superfluous power; the great fountains in the parks, the beauty and dignity of older architecture, the bell, perhaps the mighty bourdon of Notre-Dame, and a tall column in Karnak, were products of the past. Today this power is spent in the madness of producing high speed. The sonnets, I, 22–23, are similar in idea. His complaint seems to be that beauty and majesty are more important than speed, but we have lost the former to gain the latter. However, a plane in the air can be as fine as the Taj Mahal by moonlight. Tennyson could not make a poem about the locomotive, but Turner painted one beautifully in the picture "Rain, Steam and

139

Speed." Huysmans in À rebours has two fine English specimens. Hart Crane did right well by the bridge and the skyscrapers. But Rilke was a sentimental romanticist; he preferred castles by wild abysses, and without plumbing or electricity, or rent.

23.—The poet's note to this poem assigns it to the reader. Man lives in opposition to time, which is always with him, yet forever escaping him. Once a thing is lost, it becomes a treasure in the memory and therefore a permanent possession. But where we expected a welcome, we were rebuffed. Always trying to find permanency, we fall between the past, for which we are too new, and the new, for which we are already too old-fashioned. Real living lies in praising, for, after all, we are the tree of ripening fruit and the knife that cuts it. This will remind the reader of Emerson's "I am the doubter and the doubt," of Baudelaire's "Je suis la plaie et le couteau," and of Stefan George's "Ich bin der degen und die scheide / Ich bin das opfer bin der stoss."

24.—If man be only clay, what joy he gets out of it, nonetheless! Here is the evolution of cities beside "happy bays," undoubtedly, Naples, Capri, Venice which Rilke loved. Man must cling to his gods, for they will finally listen to him. Death puts us out on loan, knowing that we will one day return, more valuable by experience. But there is no mention in either the Sonnets or the Elegies of the real functions of the gods in the other world. The value of Orpheus is purely terrestrial, and the Laments seem to be the only supernatural mentors whom man meets in the next realm.

25.—A companion piece to I, 21. A landscape almost pure Barbizon is created. We think we have the spring, but when it passes we have been had. There is a breathless expectancy in this piece. It has the real mood of Vorfrühling, like Hugo von Hofmannsthal's poem by that name.

26.—The 14th Sonnet has placed man inferior to the flowers; here the birds, as in the First Elegy, are more sure of themselves than is man. In the Eighth Elegy he goes "searching his road in an ambiguous country open to the winds." But the children here, more free than man, shove their cries into the spaces in ether, like so many wedges.

140

They are wind-torn kites that have broken their strings and wander without objective through the air. Orpheus (I, 26), as the god imposing order on creation, is appealed to: he must awaken them to real life that flows like the river which bore away the god's head. In other words, they must learn to bear their part in the universal song of lamentation, and they must do it in full awareness and energetically (*rauschend*). Technically, Rilke tripped himself up here. He has chosen one of the most cacophonous sounds in his language: "Schrei," and he twangs it until one's teeth are on edge, seven times. He rubs it in by a dozen additional long *i*'s and a sprinkling of *k*'s, *ch*'s, and *s*'s. This sonnet, like somebody in Gilbert and Sullivan, "never would be missed."

27.—As the Hindu triad encompassed the creator, the preserver, and the destroyer, Siva, Rilke sees, as did the Shakespeare of the sonnets, all-destroying time that breaks or tames down all things. He ignores the fact that time is also creative and that many new things may be in process of evolution. Whereas he has often praised the wide-open "receiver," he now feels that only the doer has permanency which may be utilized by the gods. Oddly enough, in the Elegies which really include by transcension most of the material of the Sonnets, he leaves a reader in the dark about the place of the gods in his concept of the next world. See I, 22, in which "die Treibenden," the forceful characters who do things, last through the transient phases of life and in the enduring, "das Verweilende," receive their true dedication. The present sonnet is a weak version of Goethe's philosophy of the life of action.

28.—Finally (and it is time) he remembers the dead dancer again and uses her almost as a priestess of Orphism. Art is a reordering of nature, a selection which the doer believes to be the more important part of it. The girl gave herself so completely to the dance that she could not understand why nature required time to think it over before giving itself to the music of the god. He saw her dancing only once, and I seriously doubt that it was so good as he makes it seem. But if her interpretations helped him to understand the exceedingly misty and esoteric secrets of the cult, the more power to her. I feel throughout that

141

she is being used as a peg on which to hang scraps of ideas left over from the Elegies.

29.—The friend in the final line of the original of the preceding poem is, of course, Rilke himself. And his self-apostrophe continues here. The poem relates equally to I, 2, 3, and II, 1. Lines 5 and 6 here contain the germ of his idea of transformation. Explore and get knowledge ("Get wisdom and forget it not . . ."). Perhaps the most bitter experiences teach one the most. The poet must *be* the catalytic agent, or the sorcerer, that can reduce to order (a duty of the Orphic poet) the midnight confusion of the senses and make art of it. Let him now ring out like a bell, even though his music destroy him; he will grow, even by this very thing. The crossroads remind one of Peer Gynt's encounters with the Button-molder, who was, after all, only a symbol of death. As the already dying poet sings this virtual swansong, he feels that he is passing through the transiency of being; he is leaving the earth, and in the eternal change and flux of water which travels in a complete circle through cloud, rain, river, sea, vapor, back to cloud, he is at one in the state of *being* that endures this continual renewal and change without losing its integrity. He can say: Now I have become. Now I am! And if he believed that, he has given man a pattern-hope to follow.

 litotic